Escape from Southern Rhodesia before Zimbabwe

A LONDONER IN 1950S SOUTH AFRICA

To Janet, Jess
and Family.

Peter Hardy

Grosvenor House
Publishing Limited

This book is published by
Grosvenor House Publishing Ltd
Link House
140 The Broadway, Tolworth, Surrey, KT6 7HT.
www.grosvenorhousepublishing.co.uk

A CIP record for this book
is available from the British Library

ISBN 978-1-83975-785-3

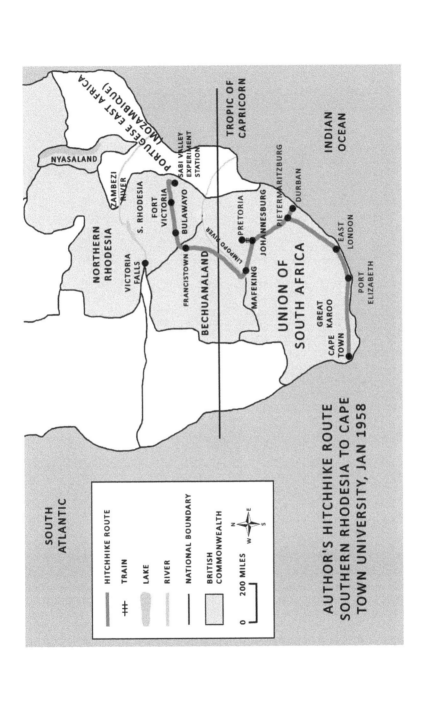

AUTHOR'S HITCHHIKE ROUTE
SOUTHERN RHODESIA TO CAPE
TOWN UNIVERSITY, JAN 1958

To My Family

Dedicated additionally to Vernon Scannell,
A famous, deceased British poet, who taught me
English Language and Literature at my school.
He encouraged in me an enquiring mind.

CONTENTS

INTRODUCTION (VOL.2)

This book (Vol.2) and the other two books in my trilogy are my impressions of places and people in Africa. These are on the theme of five years of escape and serendipity in Africa in the 1950s. This was before the old order of Empire had been seriously changed.

I was a young British immigrant working for three major southern African employers and studying at a South African university. The climax and conclusion of this experience was an overland journey from Johannesburg, South Africa, to London across Africa and Europe in 1960. I hitchhiked where possible.

I was inspired to make my African adventures by studying maps and public library books in Britain. I made my own armchair journeys into distant lands. In those fascinating regions Africa occupied a special place. This was because of the seemingly undisturbed uniqueness of its life: human, animal and vegetable.

This book relates my two thousand mile, three week hitchhike from my lonely technician post in the wilds of Southern Rhodesia to Cape Town University. I had been working in the Rhodesian Government's agricultural department, in the hot, remote, Lowveld. By thumbing I took in the best parts of South Africa.

I had been saved from death in army service in a Rhodesian civil war. I exchanged the "call up" for student life at Cape Town University.

The incomparable setting of Cape Town below Table Mountain and its university on Devil's Peak Mountain enhanced all my activities.

At Cape Town University field work was a special feature of geology involving expeditions into remote mountains and deserts. Geography and botany practical work were in the drawing office and laboratory respectively. They illustrated the richness of the Cape's environment through map exercises and the dissection and drawing of sub tropical plants. I bloodied my fingers when trying to cut a plant part with a cut throat razor. The "thin" section, more human body part than plant, was viewed under the microscope in the botany practical class.

Male and female friends from inside and outside of the university shared mountain climbs and barbecues on the beaches with me.

Another highlight was the university rag, a procession of floats through Cape Town draped with alluring female students. It was on the theme of the Russian success of launching a sputnik into space.

With the need to replenish my savings, following my academic year, I was testing explosives in Johannesburg for the gold mines! This was done in the laboratories of the largest dynamite factory in the world. The work was shared with forty technicians and industrial chemists. I had the privacy of my own little laboratory hived off the main lab where most of the scientific staff worked. I was distracted here by the erotic overtures of a female technician inductor. This caused me to make an error in my calculations in the first week. I had to defend my analyses before the chief chemist without implicating my sex pot inductor!

Explorations of the veld surrounding Joburg were made with friends from the youth hostelling club. Here I met a Jewish tailor and we resolved to return to London by an overland hitchhike trek across Africa and Europe. Dave was homesick for Britain. However, my main motive was to gain a university degree. I discovered from the personnel department at the dynamite factory that this could be obtained part time while being employed. Birkbeck College, University of London, offered this opportunity. Unfortunatey, this meant giving up a voluptuous Dutch girlfriend of fifteen. Her father, a manager in my Joburg place of work, had introduced me to her!

Since my African adventures I graduated at London University. My later career has not contradicted my opinion on my work in Africa that a non graduate can have a rich work experience.

On visits thirty five years later and subsequently, I found an Africa much more degraded than at the time of my explorations in the 1950s.

An apology to
the modern reader

This book is about my experience in South Africa, a country at the southern extremity of Africa. I worked there for two years in the 1950s. My description of this experience is as I found it at the time. It is related to the mindset that I had in those days. I like to think it is an honest account and not over-ridden by political correctness that overwhelmed the world later.

My attitude to the blacks and my white colleagues was tinged with the prevailing views of white society around me. So the terms I use to describe people are characteristic of that period. It would be dishonest to superimpose the attitudes of society today on this account. This would detract from the atmosphere of those times.

The Union of South Africa was a self governing country of the British Commonwealth dominated by whites, Europeans, but close to being changed completely by black majority rule.

South Africa was largely a conservative country preserving the niceties of pre-war Britain. It was significantly more conservative than Britain at the time, which was becoming brasher after the 2nd world war. But South Africa was developing fast, not only materially but socially as more whites entered the country.

If the reader finds my views old fashioned, and I hope not offensive, especially those of a racial and sexual nature, it reflects the times in which I found myself.

LIST OF ILLUSTRATIONS

Nyasaland and Northern Rhodesia Trek, July/August, 1959

CHAPTER 1

Rhodesia to Johannesburg

Why am I on the road?

I had spent two years working as a laboratory technician at an agricultural research station in the hot, remote Lowveld of Southern Rhodesia, now Zimbabwe. Prior to that, I carried out similar work on soils for six months in Rhodesia's modern, dynamic capital, Salisbury.

There were a number of incentives that caused me to obtain a student place at Cape Town University. I hankered for university life. I was a studious person. Cape Town had an incredibly beautiful setting of sea and mountains. This I found out when disembarking the luxury liner from Britain. The fare had been paid for by my Rhodesian Government employer.

The lonely life of the African bush had begun to impact on me. I had lost my lovely white Rhodesian girlfriend. Summons for the Rhodesian Army service was the last straw.

I was going to hitch-hike two thousand miles to Cape Town University from Rhodesia. I had already hitchhiked 300 miles in Rhodesia, after leaving my job at the Sabi Valley Experiment Station. The Rhodesian part of my journey to Cape Town is related in Book 1 of my trilogy. I was about to cross the frontier into Bechuanaland, now Botswana, in transit for South Africa.

1

Near to the Bushman

With mid-morning fast approaching, I walked along the road along which traffic would exit Southern Rhodesia and enter Bechuanaland. I had barely reached the suburbs of southwest Bulawayo when I was lucky enough to get a lift in a saloon from a white businessman.

He announced, "I'm going to Francistown."

I replied, "That will be a great help."

I recalled that the train which carried me to Salisbury from Cape Town had briefly stopped at that town which was just inside Bechuanaland.

Rhodesia's manufacturing industries were sufficiently well-developed to produce a surplus which it could export to neighbouring countries. These went to countries like Bechuanaland which were considerably less developed than Southern Rhodesia.

Ralph explained, "My business is to facilitate the movement of goods from the small-scale factories of Southern Rhodesia's Midlands to Rhodesia's neighbouring countries."

We were in Plumtree just in time to see the pupils walking down the High Street in their boaters and smart uniforms at the close of school for the day. Then in no time we had crossed the border into Bechuanaland.

Ralph dropped me in the High Street of Francistown.

"I hope you will get a good lift in the morning."

"I must get a lift otherwise I will be arrested for loitering!"

There was scarcely a white face to be seen in this town, even though it was on the only railway that passed through Bechuanaland. The Protectorate was the territory of the Bantu. There was only a sprinkling of whites, mainly administrators and professionals like hospital surgeons, water engineers and teachers at the mission schools.

Most buildings did not reach over one storey. Many did not reach that lofty height. Only the public buildings such as the police station, hospital and the like had any embellishments that did justice to the mid-20th century. Some buildings had a Victorian ring to them with wrought iron work on the veranda supports.

I bought a Coca-Cola, a universal drink in African stores, particularly where there was European influence. This was a particularly safe drink, better than using local water. I used it to wash down a chicken sandwich, a leftover from my Bulawayo pension. Following this appetiser I briefly explored the High Street. Then I settled down in my sleeping bag on the veranda of an empty house.

The next morning I walked through the dusty High Street to its southern end. I waited with anticipation for a lift under the shade of an Acacia tree, ever watchful for an approaching vehicle. This was some time in coming. But it was not what I expected. A long caravan stopped, more in the nature of an army vehicle, generously coated with the dust of the road. The driver was an African accompanied by two other Bantu, with somewhat bemused smiles on their faces. This was no doubt because they were not used to European hitchhikers.

The driver said, "I am going to Gaborone."

I remembered it was the capital and thus the administrative centre of the country. This was within spitting distance of the border with South Africa, if you disregard fifty miles shy of that important boundary.

"Thank you for giving me a lift."

As this was the first time I had a lift from an African I was apprehensive whether I would be asked for money at the end of the journey.

I settled back in the communal seat in the front of the vehicle, nearest to the passenger door. The three Africans were to my right. My precious rucksack, with my worldly goods, was lodged between my legs. I contemplated the two hundred and fifty mile journey ahead of me to the threshold of the Union of South Africa.

The bush differed little from what I had encountered in the Middleveld of the country just south of Bulawayo. More small trees than grass trundled past my window. Our speed was leisurely on the indifferent road that was Bechuanaland's major highway. This was the only road which carried vehicles from Rhodesia through the Protectorate to South Africa.

I was distracted by a slightly warm slimy jab into the back of my neck, which was repeated at regular intervals. At first I thought this was from some livestock that my companions were keeping in the business section of the caravan behind me.

One of my black companions seeing my discomfort said, "That is our large Alsatian dog. He is a guard for the caravan."

The Veterinary caravan in which I got a
lift across Bechuanaland. Jan, 1958.

The goods carried I discovered later were more than valuable. They were the lifeblood of Bechuanaland.

The driver informed me, "The vehicle belongs to the Veterinary Department. It is carrying vaccines for cattle." Abraham continued, "Operations on cows are done in the caravan when we are visiting kraals in the bush. The vet cuts open the cows to make them better."

Rearing cattle was an important activity of the Bantu in the country we passed through. These animals wandered about the bush. They fed on whatever browse they managed to find.

Unlike Southern Rhodesia there were few European farmers in Bechuanaland. The Veterinary Department was almost entirely concerned with sustaining the natives' cattle. Vaccination was a necessary activity in view of the epidemics that occasionally swept through east and southern Africa. It was in answer to one of these epidemics that the veterinary research station at Onderstepoort, Pretoria, South Africa, was set up. This later became the Veterinary Faculty of Pretoria University which my eldest daughter attended forty years after my African adventures.

The road was used throughout the year unlike most of Bechuanaland's roads. It ran parallel and a short distance from the railway. This railway I had travelled along after I arrived in Africa at Cape Town on the boat from Britain two and a half years previously.

We crossed an occasional low bridge under which water flowed, not the great flood that passed down the Sabi River in the wet season. Nevertheless this was a necessity for cattle and wildlife in the seasonally parched lands through which we passed. But the aridity of the dry season of the eastern corridor, through which we were travelling, was nothing compared with the baked lands a few score miles to the west. Here the Kalahari Desert began stretching hundreds of miles to the former German colony of South West Africa, now Namibia. This supported only the occasional bands of Bushmen. These were primitive hunter gathers that had largely disappeared from their former extensive range in Southern Africa. This was due to conflict with the superior iron age culture of the Bantu. They had swept south hundreds of years earlier. The displacement of the Bushman was continued by the alienation later of extensive areas of the veld by Europeans for farming.

Drifts (fords) where the road crossed the courses of small rivers were offshoots of the Crocodile River. This in turn was a tributary of the Limpopo. Place names in Africa, be they rivers, hills or simply stretches of countryside, got their names when Europeans first explored such areas. They associated the geographical features with some iconic wild animal they saw close by. Only the names remain to remind the modern traveller of the wild animal association, for much of such wildlife has disappeared in these areas.

As the light of day was beginning to suggest it was about to depart we arrived in Gaborone. My black driver dropped me in the centre of the town.

"Thank you very much for carrying me so many miles," I said to Abraham and his black companions. I added, "Thanks to your dog I did not fall asleep!"

With that I shook hands heartily with Abraham, Isaac and Esau.

Africans I found, particularly the rural variety, are people I feel I have some affinity with. Perhaps it is some unfathomable feeling associated with man's origins in Africa. At that time I was unaware of the work of palaeontologists like the Leakey family uncovering the origins of humans in east Africa.

Africans seemed to me uncomplicated people who lacked deviousness. To know them, no matter how fleeting, was a privilege that could not be measured. Urbanisation, materialism, familiarity with the wiles of the whites was fast depriving them of their magic. However it would be the height of naivety to fall into the trap of regarding natives, sixty years ago, as noble savages. To know something about the cruelty with which they treated other tribes when they came into conflict must modify this view. But Europeans cannot climb the moral high ground, hiding behind the pretence of being civilised. Europe had seen the utmost brutality in warfare, scarcely more than ten years before I ventured into Africa.

I surveyed the town of Gaborone. I noted the greater reliance on buildings, no matter however low and insignificant, that declared they were government departments. They were usually of the more fundamental variety, agriculture, mining, water, and veterinary services. They indicated that Gaborone was not just an ordinary dorp.

My first concern was to look for food and accommodation. I bought some bananas from a wayside stall. There was a ramshackle building just off the High Street which did not appear to be lived in. It had a veranda, just the right sort of place to set up my bedding for the night.

Early next morning I was offered a lift by a white salesman who was driving a smart saloon.

He said, "I'm going to Johannesburg. You're quite welcome to keep me company."

That city, the largest in South Africa, seemed a destination I must not miss.

I remembered from the map that a detour to the Witwatersrand, the Johannesburg conurbation, would take me away from the direct route to Cape Town. But I thought if I took the direct southerly route I would largely be following the course of the train when I first entered Africa.

I said, "A visit to Johannesburg is most welcome as it gives me an opportunity to see more of South Africa on my way to Cape Town."

South Africa entered illegally

Some fifty miles south of Gaborone we crossed into South Africa. This was the first time I had entered that country after my arrival in Rhodesia over two years previously. I was not aware of any customs and immigration formalities. This puzzled me, but I dismissed this triviality from my mind. I did not even bother to ask Jim, the driver, about the reason for this omission. Young people have a blasé attitude to authority unless it is thrust in their face. This attitude would get me into trouble.

Mafeking was soon upon us, the first South African town that I passed through of my hitchhike. But this was not my first brief visit as the Rhodesia bound train stopped here, what seemed ages ago. This was after the Union Castle boat docked at Cape Town. Mafeking, a town of only a few thousand whites, would cause me anxiety some weeks later.

This dusty place had important associations. It was here at the turn of the twentieth century that a contingent of the British Army was trapped in the town by the Boer commandos. These groups of mounted Afrikaner farmers would take on a far larger force of roineks (rednecks, Britishers). Their superior marksmanship, camouflage, and knowledge of the terrain gave them confidence. After attacks on the British positions they would melt back into the bush. This was during the early attempts of the British to take the Transvaal, the mineral rich Boer Republic the size of Britain. Here in the workings around Johannesburg was to become the most productive gold mining area in the world.

The British had a habit of pushing out predecessors in a territory. This applied to other Europeans or even non Europeans who often had been there infinitely longer. This was especially the case if there was a sniff of economic advantage. Such was the situation in South Africa.

There was the siege of Mafeking by the Boers close to the beginning of the 20th century. Now it so happened there was an enterprising British soldier called Baden Powell. He somehow managed to break through the Boer lines undetected. He penetrated their camps in disguise. He returned to the small garrison of Mafeking with invaluable information about the strength and location of enemy emplacements.

Colonel Baden Powell was enthused with his experience in South Africa. This was associated with the need to acquire bush craft when moving through the veld. This was not only because of human foes but wild animals as well. He thought it valuable to impart this knowledge to the youth of the British Empire. He was the founder of the Boy Scout movement. It therefore owes its origins, ethos, and knowledge, to the survival skills, necessary in the harsh environment of the Bushveld of southern Africa.

Stephen, my lift driver, declared, "Although I am going to Joburg I will be staying in Mafeking overnight."

I was surprised and disappointed at this announcement.

I countered, "I was hoping to get a direct lift to Johannesburg. I want to be on my way soon."

I wished Stephen, "Totsiens," goodbye in Afrikaans, as we parted company in the town. It did occur to me much later that Stephen could have pointed me in the right direction for South African passport control. Perhaps he was annoyed I did not join him at his hotel in Mafeking!

I walked as far as I could away from the centre of Mafeking on the road leading to Johannesburg. There must be nothing more confusing both to the hitchhiker and the potential lift than thumbing in the middle of a town. Here the destination of pedestrians and traffic could only be guessed at. Standing by the roadside substantially away from the delights of a town demonstrates some commitment on the part of the hitchhiker. He shows he is prepared to do some foot slogging, as his contribution to the potential journey, "a ticket to ride," so to speak.

A Citroen saloon squealed to a halt by the side of me, while I was still walking and had not even raised my thumb. I half expected to see my Sabi colleague Dave at the wheel, for the vehicle of the middle-aged bronzed driver was similar to that of my old Sabi mess mate.

"I'm heading for Johannesburg," I explained.

"Oh, you mean Joburg. Hop in. It's only two hundred miles away. We will be there in no time!"

Aaron stated, "I'm an engineer. I install and service water pumps. This is a necessary piece of machinery in mines. They are in danger of being flooded. Many rocks have groundwater saturating their nooks and crannies."

We sped along. The Bushveld gave rise to more open veld, the Highveld, since we had gained two thousand feet altitude after leaving Mafeking. Settlements passed had the true ring of the Afrikaans language, places with "dorp" at the end of their names. Much less frequently they had a combination of an Afrikaans surname and a Bantu word.

A signpost appeared to our right indicating the road to Potchestroom. This reminded me of the university where Jock, my Afrikaner mess mate, had done his agricultural science studies in the medium of Afrikaans.

My mates in the mess at Sabi, discounting my senior mess mate Richard, were all at technician level like myself. However two of them had attended university. Richard demonstrated that by gaining a degree in an appropriate subject was a passport to obtaining professional status in the Rhodesian Ministry of Agriculture. Jock and Cyril were not in this category even though they had attended university.

On returning to Britain some years later I worked in a number of laboratories. Laboratory technician posts, particularly the more senior grades, were often filled with those who had attended a science course at University. But these had left without gaining a degree. This could be due to a variety of reasons, not necessarily due to them falling short of academic demands.

I remember in my first job on returning to England from Africa a number of technicians in the laboratory being Hungarian refugees. They had left their country in 1956 due to the invasion of Hungary by the Soviet Union. They had been university students on some science related course in Budapest. There were also two English ex university students who had not completed their studies, one in medicine and another in chemistry. I felt privileged to work with them as it underlined to me the rigours of scientific studies.

CHAPTER 2

JOBURG TO THE INDIAN OCEAN

Romance in the Afrikaner's City

I have delayed the account of my arrival and exploration of Johannesburg until after a serendipitous discovery of a beautiful girl the following day!

I took the train from Johannesburg to Pretoria, a distance of about forty miles. This I had heard was a particularly picturesque city, the government administrative centre of South Africa. It was the largest stronghold of the Afrikaans speaking people.

My carriage was shared with a particularly attractive young lady. Sarie was in her late teens, a striking well proportioned popsy. She had a full bosom, brunette, and a flowery dress to enhance her figure. Sarie had a gentle voice unlike the harsh sounding words of the Afrikaners. A conversation ensued.

"I'm about to attend Cape Town University. In the mean time I'm touring South Africa, having left my job in Southern Rhodesia."

"I'm attending the Normal College in Pretoria, the teacher training college," Sarie confided.

I arranged to meet Sarie Marais later that day. In the meantime I hoped to see as much of Pretoria as possible.

The Union Buildings, the government administration buildings of the Union of South Africa, looked spectacular. They were some forty years old at the time of my visit. They opened soon after the Union came into existence. The Union was a creation resulting from the amalgamation of the Boer and British components of South Africa. This magnificent building was built in the classical style where columns featured large in deference to the ancient Greeks. It had a colonial overtone that I could not quite put my finger on. Sir Herbert Baker's masterpiece formed a great arc at the top of a number of terraced gardens in which roses were prominent.

Pretoria, the administrative capital of the Union of South Africa, has its government business done here in the Union Buildings. Jan 1958.

A large flag of the Union fluttered proudly from a high staff. It incorporated the emblems of the former Boer Republics together with a small Union Jack. This flag deferred to the main European elements that built up modern South Africa, the Afrikaners and the British. Three years later it would be scrapped. It would be replaced by a new flag when South Africa became a republic outside the Commonwealth.

In front and below the grand Union Buildings was an imposing statue of a mounted figure, General Botha, first Prime Minister of South Africa.

I met up with Sarie in a cafe in the centre of Pretoria.

I believed Sarie was of French Huguenot decent. These were people who fled France some three hundred years previously because of persecution from the predominantly Catholic French for their Protestant beliefs. South Africa among other countries benefited from the industry of the Huguenots as I did from Sarie's company.

I suggested to Sarie, "We could see a film!"

Sarie said excitedly, "I know a bioscope where we can see a film."

It was a romance with a rather catchy signature tune about Tammy being in love.

After some prolonged goodbyes of hugging and kissing we went our separate ways. It occurred to me later that I should have asked Sarie for her address and phone number so we could continue our friendship. No doubt I thought this was pointless as I was heading for Cape Town, one thousand miles away. However, as things turned out I would be near Pretoria a year later.

City of gold

I was soon in the suburbs of Johannesburg. This was no mean city. The built up area seemed to stretch for miles, a response to gold mining. Gold was found in the Witwatersrand, a ridge that stretched east-west across the south central high plateau of the Transvaal. This was South Africa's most northerly province.

Aaron dropped me in the centre of the city, the central business district, which seemed like pictures I had seen of Manhattan in New York. The high buildings formed urban canyons through which a variety of traffic streamed. I put up at the YMCA. In the morning I explored South Africa's largest city, second only to Cairo in Africa in size of population at that time. The height of the Escom building I found particularly overwhelming, nineteen stories high. London had nothing to approach this in height at the time. When I returned to England's capital it was years before this elevation was exceeded.

The Escom building was the tallest I had ever seen up to then, anywhere. Johannesburg, South Africa. Jan, 1958.

From my studies of geography it was clear that Joburg had much in common with American cities, particularly in the Midwest. The greater vehicle ownership in southern Africa as compared to Britain was illustrated by the liberal provision of parking places in the centre of Joburg. Many of these spaces were filled with privately owned cars. I had seen nothing similar to this in London on such a scale. Public transport was also provided. There were numerous double-decker buses at the bus station.

One of the main shopping streets had buildings with a general level of eight storeys high, with the latest consumer goods displayed. Doda shoe shop and OK bazaars caught my eye. The traffic was not confined to cars. Motorbikes and mopeds edged their way between the double lines of vehicles streaming in both directions.

Street scene in Johannesburg. Jan 1958.

Universal car ownership came early among the whites in South Africa. Street scene in Johannesburg.

15

There were a high percentage of white shoppers who easily outnumbered the blacks in the main shopping streets. This was explained by the greater buying power of the whites. The restriction of the movement of the blacks in certain areas of the city reserved for whites must have been an additional factor. This was in spite of the fact that even then more blacks than whites lived in the city and its environs as a whole. Today the presence of blacks in the Johannesburg conurbation as in the rest of South Africa is overwhelming. This was not only because of their fertility compared with the whites but also because many of the whites have fled the country. It is due to the passing of government from the whites to the blacks.

In my wanderings about the city I came across the Medical Research Centre building. This would not normally have excited my interest. My encounters with the snake milking men in the Sabi and particularly the one who made off with my python skin made me look twice. It was to this centre that the snake catcher sent or took their precious venom to be processed into antidote. Here the python skin I had so laboriously acquired might possibly have been treated. It no doubt found its way to adorning some woman's handbag. If only I had jammed on the Chevy's brakes faster. My trophy might have got away and its progeny might still be gracing the Zimbabwe bush with its beauty.

In addition to science related buildings, there were the usual public buildings that proud cities wish the world to take note of. These included the Law Courts and Town Hall. The former had great square towers at each corner and an impressive domed entrance. This no doubt was a busy building. In spite of the distant time I am writing about there were already murmurings of unrest among the black community. This was especially in a city which drew black workers, predominantly male, in their hundreds of thousands from every corner of the subcontinent. They worked in the mines and its associated industries. These were rural men brought up in families that eked out a living from cropping their small plots. They found themselves pulled into the concrete jungle. After their strenuous day time work they returned in the evening to their regimented residences. These were in the locations, native residential areas, on the outskirts of the white man's city. They had the promise of wealth compared with their former rural existence.

City Hall, Johannesburg, with tram outside. More whites evident then than now. Jan 1958.

I saw white city workers boarding the trains at the nearby central station on their way to their dormitories in the white suburbs. These, as I later found out, contained salubrious bungalows surrounded by large colourful gardens encouraged by the sun and warmth of the High Veld.

The next day I decided to visit such a dormitory area, a substantial town called Benoni. This had merged with Joburg like a number of towns strung along the main road and railway to the east.

The reason for this detour was to see a friend of my father's sister, Aunty Milly. This was the one who arranged for my neck to be draped with young pythons at the London Zoo when I was a boy. I believe she half hoped I would be strangled as we were both opinionated and did not get on well together. Aunty Milly, gave me the address of Dorothy, an early colleague of hers at a City of London office.

Dorothy and Fred had no children. They lived in a spacious bungalow generously surrounded by flowering gardens in a road with similar properties. The road was named after a famous British fighter plane from the Second World War. The neighbouring roads had similar names. There had been and still is an airfield nearby where allied pilots in training hung out during the 2nd world war. This was under the Empire Air Training Scheme. This reminded me of the same arrangement at the Mount Hampden Hostel where I stayed when I first arrived in Rhodesia. It was an old RAF base.

I felt at home with Dorothy and Fred and we shared experiences over tea.

Dorothy said, "Fred and I migrated to South Africa soon after we got married in 1947, the year the British royal family did a tour of southern Africa."

Dorothy asked me, "What are you going to do in Cape Town?"

When I mentioned the university she seemed puzzled that I had abandoned a career in Rhodesia!

They were a typical English couple with a home that was adorned with the usual embellishments of any middle-class home in Britain.

Fred said, "By coming to South Africa we had a major lift in our standard of living."

Reluctantly I exchanged the comfort of an armchair in Dorothy and Fred's lounge for the uncertainty of life on the road.

A proposal

I took a bus to the outskirts of Joburg on the road to Durban. I was lucky to be picked up shortly afterwards by a man in his early forties.

Ray, an English-speaking South-African, said, "I hope to be in Durban by the evening."That was music to my ears.

"Just the ticket," I replied.

I was particularly looking forward to reaching Durban because it was and is South Africa's premier seaside resort. It had celebrated sandy beaches. Its white population was sufficiently large to create a good city infrastructure, encouraged particularly by tourism.

The craggy heights of the Suikerbosrand, the Sugar Bush Ridge, some twenty miles from the edge of the Witwatersrand conurbation was passed. This sheltered some of the last predators to be found on the High Veld, including leopard. Then one hundred miles further we crossed into Natal Province. Here the country fell away from the broad rolling plains largely made up of farms growing mealies (maize), the Highveld. Natal had much more broken country that sloped one hundred and fifty miles towards the Indian Ocean.

The names of the places we passed through betrayed the origins of the Europeans that settled there. These were more recent than those Afrikaans names of the Transvaal. In Natal there were more British place names and even German ones.

To the east were the foothills of the Drakensberg, the Dragon Mountains. This is really an impressive scarp, almost a fretted cliff two thousand feet high. Here the lofty heights of Basutoland, a protectorate overseen by Britain, looked down from its plateau. It was aloof from the gathering storm that was South Africa's race relations.

Ray, as he expertly negotiated the road, seemed to be thinking, casting an eye towards a distant storm at the same time.

Suddenly he asked, "What is your driving experience in Rhodesia?"

Needless to say I left out the details of the spills I had in the Chev pickup truck. My collision with the support to the farm building and a tangle with a concrete lined ditch were glossed over.

Ray said, "I run a transport business carrying Basuto tribal products. These include handicrafts: wood carvings, hats and knitted shawls. The company returns with machinery components: parts of water pumps and other similar products."

Ray continued, "My drivers, most of whom are white, drive Land Rovers because the roads are so steep in Basutoland particularly on the eastern edge. Here the plateau is at its highest. It is much broken by the streams which rise in the heights of the Drakensberg Mountains."

It was obvious this was due to the heavy rainfall, because of the moist winds which arrived from the Indian Ocean one hundred miles away. These are forced to rise over the Drakensberg with resulting condensation. The streams soon turned to torrents in their headlong rush to the sea, joined by others with the same thing in mind. They slowed down as they reached the narrow coastal strip. But not sufficiently to blunt their erosive power for here they created river cliffs and gorges.

I realised dirt roads can be swept away by sudden surges of water. This is a hazard to any transport business in mountainous country in spite of the advantage that four wheel drive vehicles bring.

Having painted a picture of his transport business he suddenly paused, as if to give emphasis to what was to follow.

"Are you interested in becoming a driver of one of my vehicles?"

I was slow in giving him an answer, as I considered the factors involved. Not least among these was the fact that

I would be carrying valuable cargo and undoubtedly a significant amount of money. This was the takings from any transactions. However, I knew Basutoland was a little-known territory largely untouched by Europeans so the adventure of the project appealed to me. I was canny enough to realise that such a job would be a significant break in the continuity of the theme of my career. It had no scientific component. The overriding consideration was I would soon be a student at the University of Cape Town. There hopefully I would further my interests in science and geography.

Money of course is uppermost in most people's minds but I would not place this above my interests in environmental subjects. So I declined Ray's kind offer. I never did visit the Drakensberg and Basutoland. However, my eldest daughter Clare made up for my deficiency. She went on a climbing expedition there with some fellow students from Pretoria University four decades later!

Native huts became more numerous the further we penetrated south into Natal. The Bantu advanced across southern Africa, from the edge of the great tropical rain forest of the Congo, millennia before. They were not only stopped by the sea but the amenable nature of the region to pasture and cultivation. This was because of the heavier rainfall of Natal compared with the land further inland in the Transvaal. In consequence the rural native population of Natal was higher than most other parts of South Africa. This was reflected in the numerous African names which were associated with landscape features, particularly with the rivers

Ray confided, "I live in Pinetown, a satellite of Durban, from which it is about ten miles away."

It served as a commuter's residential area. With the spectacular growth in the urban area of Durban, since I passed through more than sixty years ago, Pinetown has become part of the urban sprawl of the city.

The Indian Ocean

Ray kindly dropped me in the centre of Durban.

He said, pointing to an unobtrusive building, "That is a relatively cheap but wholesome bed and breakfast establishment."

The following day made it clear that Durban was a bustling place. This was not least explained by the South African and Rhodesian tourists, with no doubt a generous sprinkling of international visitors.

Durban exceeded Cape Town in the amount of sea traffic that its harbour attracted. It had the largest port in Africa. I walked along the promenade. Cargo ships were being unloaded along the quayside by cranes. The grotesque shapes of the cranes reminded me of the visitation of Martians in the "*War of the Worlds.*" But the bustle of the harbour was not confined to the arrival and dispatch abroad of goods like sugar, derived from the Natal cane fields. Liners arrived and departed, not least those of the Union Castle Line. Many did not turn round at Cape Town for a return to Europe. They continued along the South African coast to Durban and beyond.

On returning towards the centre of the city along the promenade I came across the colourful sight of rickshaw Zulu boys. These were plying their trade along the road adjacent to the promenade. To call the "drivers" of these fascinating vehicles "boys" would appear as an insult to whites newly arrived from Europe. But I considered myself a southern African at that moment in time. The "drivers" of the rickshaws were pullers. I imagined it needed some physical strength to set these two wheelers in motion. These were large black men with rippling muscles, ornately dressed, with huge cattle horns on their heads backed with long ostrich feathers. They plied a brisk business from the tourist trade.

I knew there was a large Asian population in Durban, the largest concentration of these people in the subcontinent.

Rickshaw drivers. Magnificent specimens of men.
To call them 'boys' seemed an insult.
Durban, South Africa. Jan1958.

I wondered whether the idea of the rickshaw had come from them as it is common in India.

The Asians of South Africa I discovered were not regarded by the whites as much better than the blacks. The blacks had long lived in separate areas to the whites but this was also true of the Asians. Even the beaches were demarcated with respect to ethnicity together with benches along the seafront. But there was an Indian at one time resident in South Africa who would turn the tables on this state of affairs. One trained as a lawyer who went by the name of Gandhi who later moved to India. He was instrumental in kicking out the British in the Indian subcontinent in what is now India and Pakistan. The Indian people could then determine their own destiny and not defer to foreigners. Actions like this had a knock-on effect. The British Empire, or more precisely the British

Commonwealth which succeeded it, got the message that native people did not want to be ruled by the whites.

I walked along the beach, pristine sands washed by the Indian Ocean. This ocean had a long fetch, the distance of open sea to which the coast was exposed. It was four thousand miles to the shores of Western Australia and a similar distance to South America and about half that distance to Antarctica. Winds travelling over these colossal distances had no difficulty in whipping up the waves when they decided to blow. There was the need for hunky lifesavers ever watchful at their posts along the sands.

But this was not the only danger that such waters could bring. Occasionally bathers would spot the unmistakable "sail" breaking the water. Not a boat or even an unwary submarine but the fin of one of nature's most feared creatures, a shark! This predator cruised the shallows in search of some tasty, meaty, morsel! Along the most vulnerable shores nets were strung in the water to deter such ferocious predators.

My mind was deflected from such matters by the sight of popsies. This was a South African term for attractive young ladies. They were sporting themselves on deck chairs.

Very young ladies on Durban's beach, 1958.

I called out to one girl, "You are looking very brown."

She smiled but did not reply. Did she regard me as a cruiser like the sharks?

Though I was young, barely twenty two, I found a lot of the white girls on that beach too young. They were possibly in their early teens! This was quite a revelation for it made me wonder how I would find the female students at Cape Town University!

During the evening I consulted my map to see how I could progress in the Cape Town direction. It was clear that I must backtrack to Pietermaritzburg, some forty miles inland, which I had passed through only a couple of days before. This was in order to get onto the main road to Cape Town. There was a coastal road threading its way west which could have shortened my journey. However, I rejected this short cut because it seemed unlikely to have through traffic.

I got a bus to the northern outskirts of Durban. I was lucky in getting a lift in a smart saloon. This was driven by a tall, slim professional looking man in his thirties who was going to East London. This was about three hundred miles away.

From Pietermaritzburg, near Durban, I had a lift in this
smart saloon to East London, 300 miles away.

John said, "I hope to be at my destination before nightfall."

I said with a smile, "You are promising me a substantial chunk of my projected journey to Cape Town!"

Zulu and Xhosa lands

John kindly stopped at the occasional lay-by, or rather a patch of gravel which answered for such a term. The road was adequately surfaced for its full width unlike the half widths on the main roads in Southern Rhodesia. There was none of the Kentucky Fried Chicken type pull in establishments we have today by the side of the main roads in Britain. Compensating for this the minor towns had more discreet eating places. These one could associate with the very English genteel establishments of Agatha Christie's novels.

Much of the route was undulating particularly rugged to the north, the foothills of the Drakensberg. These reached four thousand feet or more in the distance rivalling the Scottish Highlands in altitude. But beyond these hills, out of sight, were the dramatic precipices of the Drakensberg Mountains.

Patches of woody vegetation clung onto the lower slopes of the hills. They had managed to avoid being grubbed up in order to extend the scattered native maize cultivation. But such vegetation was likely to be decimated by the foraging of the Zulu and Xhosa wandering sheep and goat herds. These branches of the Bantu had a history of warlike raids. This was not only on neighbouring native people but also Europeans when the Boer's had come too close to their territory. Later the British suffered some reversals at the hands of the Zulu impis in their advance into South Africa.

Above the mixture of scrub and mealie field patches, with the occasional collection of native huts (kraals), was a drab brown belt. This was reminiscent of moorland. Here and there below the moorland were groups of natives weeding the patches of maize with badzas (native hoes). The indifferent maize merged into the scrub, which was possibly fallow from a previous cycle of cultivation.

We sped past natives weeding their patches of cultivation.

Black women were conspicuous among these farm labourers as they were usually in any native farming. This was at odds with the European agricultural enterprises where male natives were used as labour. This was my experience on the experimental farms of Sabi, Rhodesia. Native men were attracted by the financial reward economy of whites. The Europeans in turn benefited from the steady consistent labour of the black men in a plantation type situation. Native women would be less suitable in these circumstances. The reason was not only because they were not so strong but also because of the demands of rearing children and looking after their men.

In places we had to slow down as a river valley was approached. The road would zigzag down the slope to cross a bridge. This afforded a brief glimpse of water swiftly making its way to the sea. Almost without exception these rivers had native names, Zulu and later Xhosa, as we entered the Transkei, the stronghold of the Xhosa nation.

The map indicated that none of these rivers had come more than eighty miles or so before they entered the sea. They mostly rose just below the Drakensberg, essentially the southern boundary of Basutoland and the comparable highlands that extended west.

Most of our journey since leaving Maritzburg had been in the Cape Province. It was the largest administrative area of the Union of South Africa occupying the south-western part of that country. The road we were following was more picturesque than much of South Africa further inland.

Entering the Transkei proper the native population density was clearly greater than what I had seen previously. This was illustrated by the myriad of kraals. These included enclosures for livestock, be they cattle or goats, which were driven into their corrals with the approach of night.

I remembered the colourful menu cards embellished with South African scenes of traditional native life. These I encountered at dinner on the *Edinburgh Castle* liner on my voyage from UK to South Africa. They showed scenes from the Transkei. Here native women were shown bare to the waist displaying their assets to full advantage. They were pounding away with a giant piece of wood the maize grain in a tall section of hollowed tree trunk to make mealie porridge. Unfortunately I never got to see this erotic scene in the flesh. In reality, at that time, the native women invariably covered up with discarded European clothes.

Maize is not a native of Africa but of the Americas and was introduced at the penetration of the African continent by Europeans. It had a phenomenal effect on the native population, particularly in southern Africa, for it was relatively easily cultivated. It provided a great increase in the food supply and consequently the population. This caused the degradation of the environment. Much of the land has soils that are easily eroded by heavy rain. When they dry out they can be whipped up by the winds so that desertification is a threat to much of Southern Africa.

Troubled sleep on the promenade

We arrived in East London in late afternoon.

John said, "I'll drop you close to the town centre."

I noted this was near the promenade. In the remaining light it was clear that the promenade like those of seaside resorts in Britain had benches and shelters. The latter appealed to me for they were only open to the front and had a roof. The bench inside was more than long and wide enough to accommodate someone like me fully stretched. I decided to spend the night in his way immersed in my sleeping bag.

This was the European part of the beach, as the notices make clear, "NO BLACKS" in English and Afrikaans. Such a notice would be unthinkable today. In the early 1990s apartheid, the separating of the races, came to an end with black majority rule.

In my beach shelter I eat a sandwich and chewed on a piece of biltong (dried meat), which I always contrived to carry on me. I noted the last whites on the promenade had dissolved away .This was the cue for me to coil up in my sleeping bag with my rucksack as a pillow. One of the straps of the rucksack was wound around my wrist. This was not the most comfortable of ways to spend the night. However, I would save a significant amount of money by not putting up at a more substantial lodging. Some would say sleeping in this way was tantamount to putting one's life, or at least one's belongings, at risk. But it should be remembered that South Africa was relatively crime free at that time. That is as far as whites were concerned compared with today. Now it is said even to stop at traffic lights on quiet nights puts you at risk from muggers or worse.

Johannesburg today is reputed to be the murder capital of the world. However, East London, at that distant time seemed a quiet place, halfway between Durban and Cape Town. I was taking a calculated risk dossing down in that shelter on the promenade. I had the rhythmic sound of the surf echoing in my ear, the good one that is, whenever I lifted it from my rucksack. It was my custom to sleep with my good ear glued to my pillow. This was an attempt to shut out distractions, at least the ones that make sounds. The advantage of this, in the case of the East London shelter, was that I was facing the promenade and the beach. My back was protected by the rear of the shelter. Street lights on the adjacent coastal road were at rather wide intervals. They were therefore not disturbing. They afforded some view of the scene ahead. This was an advantage in detecting anything that approached from the front. I was a light sleeper.

I persuaded myself that I was safe in a white area. Blacks usually lived in locations, dwelling areas, far removed from white areas. They were usually on the outskirts of the towns. Additionally black areas often had a buffer between them and a white area. This might be a railway, industrial estate or similar land use.

South African police were overwhelmingly Afrikaners. They were either respected, mistrusted, or feared, depending on whether you were an Afrikaner, English speaking white or black respectively. The police made regular patrols. This was done in their conspicuous vehicles, revolvers prominently displayed in their holsters, and sjamboks (whips), close to hand!

There were "poor whites," so-called. They were often of Afrikaner extraction. They were people who had fallen on hard times because of rapid agricultural mechanisation, industrialisation and urbanisation of South Africa. These factors displaced them from rural areas and sucked them into the larger towns and burgeoning cities. Indeed many of the blacks experienced the same process. These proverbial Dick Wittingtons did not find the pavements lined with gold. This was even in a country swimming with mineral wealth. Might therefore the SAP (South African Police) mistake me for one of these characters while I was snoozing on my bench? They might hurl insults in Afrikaans at me like "Voertsek!", "be off dog!" A worse fate might be to bundle me into one of their notorious jails? In fact my brush with security officers was just around the corner!

CHAPTER 3

GARDEN ROUTE

Bushmen and mermaids

Here I fast forward my account to relate a strange story.

A few miles west of Knysna Forest we passed through an area known as Wilderness. Here I persuaded Jeremy, my hitch-hike driver, to make a stop or two to appreciate the variety of its scenery and habitats. A view from a coastal high point revealed waves breaking on sand and rocks. Behind the beach was a small settlement with widely spaced houses and bungalows.

The Garden Route afforded magnificent views
of the Indian Ocean coast. Jan 1958.

Jeremy explained, "This place is one of the most desirable spots in the whole of Southern Africa to live, especially for those who are retired. One of its attractions is there has been a rumour going about, well in excess of one hundred years. This suggested mermaids frequented the sea and lagoons around the settlement. This rumour was given more credence when Bushmen rock paintings were discovered in a neighbouring cave. The rock walls featured human forms with fishes' tails as well as the other attributes of the female figure. This discovery was made not long ago. The Bushmen left these titillating aberrations many years before the first Europeans settled in the area round about the close of the 18th century. The Bushmen are no longer found in these parts. Therefore there was no collusion between the Bushmen and the whites. The Bushmen were acute observers of nature. They knew which species of plants were edible and which were poisonous and of course they knew about animals around them. They were bush pharmacists par excellence. Among their pharmaceutical knowledge they knew that some plants could be used as narcotics. This could enliven their dancing and observational powers regarding mermaids!"

One of my daughters became a pharmacist years later. She said to me, "I have great respect for herbal remedies. It's a pity there isn't more recognition of these treatments in modern conventional medicine."

Seaside in East London

I return to the chronological order of my explorations.

So after a fitful sleep on a promenade bench I found that dawn had well and truly passed. I visited a departmental store in the town to get spruced up, and had an egg and chips in a neighbouring cafe. On returning to the promenade I walked towards the docks. There were some people on the promenade already, some barely putting one foot before the other. A few were striding out in a business like fashion. There is nothing like sea air, surf and sand to put one in an optimistic mood.

The only ship I saw moving while I was in East London was a tug entering the harbour. Ships have always held a fascination for me. However, I never had thoughts of requesting the Navy as an option for my potential national service. Here I am referring to Britain, as Rhodesia did not have a Navy, no need because it was landlocked! My attitude to the Navy was that you did not join the Navy "To see the world" as the advert goes. Even in my late teens I realised most of the time you were in the Navy you were at sea and probably below decks.

East London seemed a curious name to give a resort on the South African coast. What I had seen of the South African town was the reverse of anything I had seen in the East End of London, England. It was clean, well laid out, and next to the magnificent Indian Ocean. But in spite of that the black locations, residential areas for Africans on the edge of the town, had experienced recent unrest. This happened in a number of urban areas in the Union at that time. It was "The writing on the wall," a taster of far more trouble in the years to come in race relations in southern Africa.

A bilingual nation

I walked through the white suburb of East London straddling the main road to Port Elizabeth. Midday was nearly upon me. A station wagon stopped in answer to my thumb and I was on my way. The English-speaking South African driver seemed hardly older than me. He was impressed with the distance I had covered from Rhodesia. English-speaking Europeans predominated on the south coast of South Africa. Afrikaans speakers occurred more in the rural inland areas of the Cape Province, the Orange Free State and the Transvaal, provinces of South Africa.

At the time of my residence the majority of the Afrikaners were bilingual. They could speak English if they wanted. However, many of the white English speakers could not understand Afrikaans. This applied mainly to the older citizens. However, both languages were official and taught in schools. The consequence of this was that South African European schoolchildren had the advantage of being bilingual. They fulfilled the need for a foreign language in their school leaving certificate and matriculation to a South African University with relative ease. Everything in South Africa was in the two languages. If you were young you could not help picking up the two languages. This contrasted with the situation in Britain. Here the majority of children found the acquiring of a foreign language such as French more demanding.

Clues in geographical names

On leaving the outskirts of East London, South Africa, we almost immediately passed through a small settlement called Cambridge. As the road twisted to gain height we met dorps with German names.

Potsdam was followed by Berlin, "These reflected the origins of settlers in the 19th century," Harry, my driver pointed out.

The road maintained a distance of some thirty miles from the coast. The countryside was pleasantly hilly. We descended from time to time in order to cross rivers. These had risen in mountains some one hundred miles away in the interior of Cape Province. The rivers had names like the Great Fish and Bushman's River. The latter name reminded me that the primitive Bushman, a hunter gatherer, once extended his range to the coast of South Africa. He retreated due to incursions of the Bantu from the north and the white man from the south. This had caused him to move hundreds of miles north-west to the fringes of the Kalahari Desert.

We passed through the small town of Grahamstown, a pleasant place which in spite of its size had a relatively famous university. Rhodes University was where Cyril, my Sabi, Rhodesia, mess mate, had done some study.

In no time we were in Port Elisabeth, which as the name suggests was where we joined the coast. I was disappointed that the five hundred mile road journey from Durban to Port Elizabeth had only afforded me views of the sea at East London. Port Elizabeth had a major port which the Union Castle liners would put into as their first port of call after Cape Town on their way to Durban.

The next day saw me on the road again just outside PE. I was lucky to get a lift within a short time from a tall, slim, English-speaking South African, in his forties. He drove a saloon and was dressed in the traditional way of male South Africans in open neck shirt, shorts and long socks. The latter should have reached just beneath the knee. I noticed whenever we stopped to view the landscape that his socks were invariably down. One was halfway down and the other completely down. This problem I frequently had with my long, elasticated, southern African socks.

Geomorphology explains scenery

The scientific appreciation of scenery is called geomorphology, a branch of geology, the study of rocks.

The road swung away from the coast, with hilly country appearing to the north and then swung back skirting the coast to Jeffrey's Bay. This afforded views of the Indian Ocean rollers coming in to meet the shore near Cape St Francis. The road provided splendid views of the margin between sea and land. It undulated backwards and forwards, a view of the interior hills and mountains and then a view of the sea.

Jeremy said, "We are on the Garden Route, one of the most scenic drives in the whole of South Africa."

We passed lagoons, shallow coastal lakes trapped by sandbars. This was due to the complications of water movement carrying sediment where a river enters the sea. Additionally there was long shore drift. This was the movement of sand and pebbles down the coast by currents moving parallel with it. The waters dropped their load where the current slackened due to some obstacle in its path.

Not far outside Port Elizabeth the road descended and bent, descending again passed the bend. A sure sign we were approaching a river crossing. But this was no ordinary river because it had cut a deep gorge.

I exclaimed, "Please slow down Jeremy. I want to see this amazing spot."

The gorge produced by the Storms River did not have the classic clean vertical sides of a canyon, but a jagged scene of interlocking spurs. Where the river zigzagged, and each component of the zigzag partially concealed the other when viewed from the bridge. The whole vista was covered in native bush. This was a jumble of moderately sized trees and shrubs, which had avoided the slash and burn scenario of native agriculturalists. The terrain was too rugged for cultivation or grazing by domestic animals.

So awesome was the scene that I gained from the moving car that I was unable to appreciate the bridge fully as we passed over it. I did get a glimpse as we first approached its span on the final descent of the road before cruising over the Storms River. Seeing the bridge was a revelation. It was one of the most beautiful I had seen in its spectacular geometrical lines of concrete and steel. It had simplicity, no excess of material. It was built for utility, pure and simple, and did this magnificently. The qualities of strength, power and beauty was displayed in this recently built bridge. This civil engineering feat sent out a message that South Africa was a country of substance.

Plettenberg Bay was a scenic high point on the Garden Route. Approaching and leaving the Plettenberg Bay area revealed a wealth of landscapes. There was the beach with the lines of waves seemingly queuing up to tumble on the sands in successive breaks of white surf. Rocks impeded this progress momentarily causing the waves to leap upwards and crash down as fast as they could. They were seemingly in a hurry to catch up with the rest of the line of waves from which they had broken rank. At such locations I would gain these impressions from the speeding car. I reinforced them in more detail when we stopped. This was occasionally to take in the panorama that unfolded below us from some high vantage point.

The road and lay-bys where we stopped were frequently free of vehicles.

I uttered, "Jeremy you are king of the road in this immense country! There is little traffic or settlement to slow you down. You would be envied by drivers in Europe."

At this Jeremy smiled.

Magical rain forest

There were places where the road swung inland for a number of miles. Such an area was Knysna, or more especially Knysna Forest. The high rainfall in these parts was due to the rain bearing winds from the Indian Ocean, some ten miles away. Forced upwards they were caused to shed their moist load on the coastal uplands. Combined with the warm subtropical climate this had resulted in the only extensive indigenous forest in the whole of southern Africa. It extended some sixty miles east- west and twenty miles north-south. Fortunately the road passed through some of its length. This afforded a good opportunity to appreciate its nature. Good that is as far as you can view such a rare scene from a moving car.

I asked Jeremy, "Could you please stop where convenient? I want to take a closer look at this unusual forest."

Some of the trees were of considerable size, not only in height, perhaps exceeding eighty feet, but also in girth. Mixed with these were lower trees and shrubs. There were lianas, creeping plants, which hung from the branches. Epiphytes, perhaps orchids, grew on the branches and in their axils, where the branches joined the trunks of the trees. They didn't have roots. They relied on the moist air for water.

Knysna, a rare subtropical forest in South Africa.

Coating the trees' stems and branches was a thick layer of mosses and where they could not gain a hold there were lichens. These were circular areas a few inches across. Different species had different colours. Some lichen species flattened themselves against the trunk but others were raised above the surface like leaves. These plants are an amalgam of a fungus and alga, each bringing a different form of nutrition to the structure. They are curious plants, plants because the algal part is capable of photosynthesis, making carbohydrates, sugars, by combining carbon dioxide and water in the presence of sunlight. The fungal part of the lichen is capable of breaking down dead organic matter, providing nutrients for the lichen. This is a self sustaining arrangement necessary in the harsh environment of a tree trunk or rock. Lichens are therefore true pioneers.

Lichens have no roots. Water is obtained from that which falls on them from rain, or more particularly drains down the trunk of the host tree.

The profusion of different species of lichen was an indicator that this area was free of air pollution. In the presence of such air pollutants as sulphur and nitrogen dioxide only the most tolerant lichen species, as in industrial areas of Johannesburg, persist.

Mosses and lichens grew in abundance in such areas as Knysna because of the high humidity. Moist air was trapped within and below the tree canopy and not allowed to dry out appreciably because of frequent rain.

In the shrub and herb layer were ferns. Their fronds heavy on their undersides with spore bearing structures which enabled the plant to disperse through the forest.

The Knysna Forest was famous for its stinkwood tree which was valued for furniture making. Fortunately Knysna was a protected area so what cutting was done was judicial.

Jeremy exclaimed, "A herd of elephants inhabits the Knysna Forest!"

I retorted, "Sensible for them we have seen none. Otherwise people might be tempted to take pot shots at them from the road!"

Elephants are very adaptable and occur in a wide range of habitats. They are generally associated with the African savanna, a fairly open area of grass and scattered trees and shrubs of variable density. Elephants can also inhabit dense forest. This was illustrated by Knysna Forest and the tropical rainforest of the Congo where they frequent well used trails which link up with glades. Sometimes they live in almost impenetrable thickets. Impenetrable that is to a man as in the Addo Nature Reserve close to the Garden Route that our vehicle followed. They also occur in desert areas such as South West Africa, now Namibia.

Development versus conservation

The settlement of Wilderness was very close to the Sea. The waves due to rising sea level could undermine and demolish properties closest to the shore.

One viewpoint near Wilderness showed where the coast took on a much more rugged appearance. Here a steep vegetated rocky slope ended in a headland. Waves broke on its extremity, which marked the side of the bay. A third of the way up this slope, cut out of the rock, could be seen in the distance the continuation of our road. It disappeared into a tunnel.

Big, relatively new countries, those that had not been settled by progressive people for long, like South Africa, produced great civil engineering projects. Development of this kind was illustrated by the road tunnel before me and the Storms River Bridge passed not long before. I marvelled at such things and my experience in soil mechanics in Rhodesia made me feel part of pushing the frontier forward. But in this there was conflict with the natural world. Any aspiring geographer/earth scientist like me was increasingly aware of this as the years, decades, half a century, elapsed. Development was at war with the natural world. This realisation was fostered in my case largely by my African experience. I hoped that my student days at Cape Town University would enhance my knowledge and appreciation of the environment. Perhaps it would equip me to further my interests in these subjects.

Yet another view point in the same area showed a river flowing through a valley with steep sides, a gorge. Here the road clung to the riverbank. There was a road bridge near where the river entered the sea. By such a splendid view point some enterprising individual had built a bungalow with the universal stoep (veranda). It defied gravity on the mountainside.

"I would love to have a summer house here, Jeremy sighed."

The rivers were short that came down from the Drakensberg Mountains, but often spectacular where they entered the Indian Ocean. South Africa, Jan 1958.

The problem with such magnificent coastal scenery is that there is always the threat of pepper pot development, scattered residencies sometimes jerry-built. This happened in the 1930s along England's coast. The planning departments, if they existed, were then much more relaxed about such things.

Another vista along the coast was of a less rugged aspect. Here the estuary of a river had numerous sandbanks, a characteristic of rivers when they enter the sea. The river's speed was checked and deposition of the finer particles of their load took place. The sandbanks had cut off water from the sea creating lagoons, containing mats of vegetation. These harboured plentiful bird life. No doubt the birds were attracted by the wealth of aquatic invertebrates, small water creatures without backbones. In such situations there is often a gradation of salinity in the water, ranging from fresh water of the river with no salt, to seawater with plenty. A variety of mixtures of saltwater and freshwater occur encouraging a wealth of plants and aquatic creatures. Each had their preference for water of different salinities.

We arrived in the small settlement of George, a short distance, from the coast. It was about halfway between Port Elizabeth, which I had left earlier that day, and my final destination Cape Town.

I said to Jeremy, "Please drop me here as the evening light is beginning to fade. I like to see the countryside in the light. I can't thank you enough for the lift. You have shown me the best of South Africa."

Jeremy replied, "Thank you for interesting company."

I managed to find a small bed and breakfast establishment. This was not too difficult as the town was in one of the premier tourist areas of South Africa.

In the morning I was on my way again, for my lift came quickly. Lucky again! My driver, Stephen, a middle aged businessman with a slight German accident was heading for Cape Town that day. This was some three hundred and fifty miles away.

The road afforded a distant view of Mossel Bay, a major indentation of the coast. We skirted the small coastal town of the same name. We were both anxious to reach the "Tavern of the Seas", Cape Town.

Explorers of coastal South Africa

Stephen informed me, "The whole southern coast of South Africa is littered with wrecks of ships that had come to grief on rocks. This was over a period of some four hundred years. Many of them sunk during the days of sail."

The Portuguese made their probing along the coast of the southern limits of the continent of Africa in the late 15th and early 16th centuries. They had rounded the Cape of Good Hope, close to where Cape Town would arise. Then making a great leap of faith sailed into the unknown, as if they had not been doing that before. Much of the planet south of Portugal was unexplored. But the unknown this time was much further from land than hitherto. They sailed across the Indian Ocean! They arrived in the lands of their dreams, the Far East, where they enriched themselves with precious spices, fabrics, not to mention jewels.

The early Portuguese explorers were ignorant of the fact that the interior of the southern African continent, they had just skirted, had wealth unimaginable. That would cause the riches of the East Indies to pale into insignificance in the centuries to come. These intrepid explorers had no means of exploiting the interior of southern Africa. That would have to wait much later for others to follow, mostly non-Portuguese Europeans.

Stephen informed me, "The Portuguese navigators liked Mossel Bay and made landfall there."

I said, "It is one thing to be impressed by viewing a coast from a ship but another to go ashore and make a go of settling there."

It was a Portuguese explorer who first rounded the Cape of Good Hope. He crept tentatively along the waters lapping the southern extremity of the African continent. He was Bartolomeu Dias who did it in 1488. Ten years later Vasco da Gama explored further east along the coast. He appeared to be impressed with his view of the country around present day Durban which he saw on Christmas Day and so named it Natal. This name has stuck for more than five hundred years, up to the present!

Prelude to Cape Town

From Mossel Bay the road struck inland and maintained a distance of about forty miles from the coast. This route was compensated by distant views of the mountains. As the miles mounted and the sun sank lower I reconsidered reaching Cape Town the same day. True, there was no doubt we could reach Kaapstad by evening. I did not fancy walking about a large city in the dark. In the mid twentieth century, Cape Town and the other cities of South Africa did not have violence on the scale of the 21st century. However, as I passed through there was restlessness in the black quarters of South African cities. This could have spilled over into the markedly white centres and suburbs.

I questioned the wisdom of seeking accommodation in the dark in a city of three quarters of a million people. Besides I wanted to see the scenery of the final sector of my two thousand mile journey across the subcontinent. I decided to stop short of the legislative capital of the Union at an appropriate dorp. This settlement should be within easy striking distance of the "Tavern of the Seas."

The light was still good as we came to a region where the mountains crowded close to the road. Below them was the small town of Caledon.

I asked Stephen, "Could you please drop me in the centre? I want to have enough time tomorrow to see the mountainous approach to Cape Town and to sort out accommodation in that city."

Stephen nodded in agreement. He wished me well and left me waving on the pavement.

In no time I found a pension that seemed to meet my needs. My room was all the more appealing as it had pictures of the early days of South Africa. There were scenes of the Great Trek, when the Boers penetrated the interior of the sub continent. Their earnestness to escape the acquisition of the lands immediately around Kaapstad by the British had no bounds.

My breakfast too was enlivened not only by eggs and bacon but boerwors, the sausage traditional to the Afrikaans speaking people. In the past it was packed inside with the meat of the veld, wild game.

I walked through the town towards the western outskirts in the direction of my final destination. I had risen early so I hoped I would get a lift in good time. This would enable me to suss out accommodation in Cape Town before the day ended.

My lift materialised quite quickly, a volkswagen driven by a weather beaten, tall, slim man in his late twenties. Jack was a manager with a wine producing company just north-east of Cape Town.

Most young Europeans in southern Africa seemed slim and healthy sixty years ago in contrast to the situation in Britain today with the explosion in obesity. Additionally they were not round shouldered. This is ascribed to a sedentary lifestyle crouching over a computer or play console. But I am not exempt from this. Typing this account of my African experience has encouraged my sorry appearance!

It might seem surprising that these observations on the health of southern African whites, at that distant time, concluded that they were in good health. Large numbers of whites relied on their cars for just getting around the block. They had an advanced American life style. Additionally they were waited on hand and foot by black servants. I cannot place myself on the moral high ground in that respect because I enjoyed the services of attentive domestic servants. This was when I was living in the bachelors mess in the Lowveld of Rhodesia! Counteracting this was that most white southern Africans spent a great deal of their time in the open air under the glorious sun. More to the point they played sport.

Half of the sixty mile journey from Caledon to Cape Town was passed through rugged country. Much of it was covered in what in England would be called heathland. This consisted of heather like shrubs of many different species. The Afrikaans term for the heathland plant community around Cape Town is *fynbos*, occupying a very small fraction of South Africa's area. It has an extraordinary range of plant species including the iconic protea. These are flowering plants of extraordinary beauty, associated with South Africa more than any other plant species. At the time of writing these sentences proteas were in great demand in Britain. Nelson Mandela, the native South African who led the revolution of the blacks against the oppressive white nationalist regime had just died!

Cape of Good Hope

Getting ever closer to my final destination, the ground seemed to give way to produce an escarpment known as the Hottentot Holland Mountains.

Jack said pointing, "That is a distant view of False Bay, a gulf of the sea thirty miles across. It penetrates in-land by an equal amount. Across its breadth can be seen the rugged Cape Peninsula terminating in the fabled Cape of Good Hope. This is one of the most southerly tips of the African continent."

Cape Town & Cape Peninsula. The Southern extremity of Africa reached. Cape of Good Hope in far distance. Jan 1958.

The escarpment of the Hottentot Holland Mountains was due to earth movements along a fault, a crack in the Earth's crust, produced eons of time previously. I shifted my gaze, from our vantage point, from the sea to the south west, to the Cape Flats. This was an area of agricultural holdings, *vlei* (marsh) and lakes as well as shanty residences for poor blacks. Beyond this were the suburbs of Cape Town, twenty miles away, ever encroaching on this flat area.

Descending the slope we skirted the small industrial town of Somerset West. This place would have considerable significance in my life unbeknown to me at that moment.

I told Jack, "I have received joining instructions for the university. These include a list of accommodation used by students. One particular address has caught my eye, the Devonshire Hill Hotel. The attached map shows it is in Rondebosch."

Jack explained, "Rondebosch is a suburb of Cape Town. It is on the mountain edge just above which the university is located. I will drop you in Rondebosch as I am early. It will not be too much of a detour for me." Not only did he drop me in Rondebosch, but more conveniently outside the Devonshire Hill Hotel! Jack said as we parted, "I wish you well in your studies," with a slightly incredulous expression on his face.

I reminded him, "No matter what the future might hold. I have completed the two thousand mile journey to Cape Town from Rhodesia. This is thanks to the kindness of people like you!"

CHAPTER 4

SETTLING INTO CAPE TOWN

A Student's Hotel

Passing through a large garden planted with subtropical shrubs and trees, for Cape Town has a Mediterranean climate, I approached the Devonshire Hill Hotel. I crossed a lawn to an imposing flight of broad stone steps. On either side was a mature palm tree. Their foliage stretched out to form an arch. The hotel was of substantial size, at least in length, but limited to one storey high. It appeared bright and airy due to the sun reflected on its brilliant white-wash.

My hotel in Cape Town. Too good for a student! 1958.

I ascended the steps shouldering my rucksack, the straps of which were beginning to dig into my shoulders. I should not have complained to myself about this slight discomfort. I had done very little walking during my mammoth hitchhike from the Sabi Valley. The generosity of my lifts enabled me to avoid that indignity. That was to be rectified in the months to come.

Pushing open the heavy door at the top of the garden steps I entered a large foyer. I was aware of the dimming of light and temperature in contrast to the intensity outside. There was a limited number of arm chairs and a reception desk to my right, but no one was about. This gave me time to consider what I was about to do. Was it appropriate for a prospective student of very limited means to contemplate staying at a hotel? This was while he pursued his studies in grand halls of learning. These were seemingly half way up a mountain, Devil's Peak.

On striking the bell on the highly polished desk I thought I would soon find out the answer to this little problem. Anyway the booklet on accommodation from the University listed the hotel as a possible place of residence. But what kind of student had Cape Town University in mind when recommending such accommodation? Students are well known to vary in their means. They range from virtually penniless to fabulously rich thanks to the bank of mum and dad. The term "hotel" was somewhat off putting rather than hostel or even hall, for a poor student.

True, I had saved up some money in Rhodesia, but it did not amount to much. It was stowed safely away in the Standard Bank of South Africa. I was trying to stay at a hotel for an indefinite period while I pursued my studies. Some would say this was at the end of the world. There was nothing beyond this extreme southerly tip of Africa. The snowy wastes of Antarctica did not count for much. In between the seething unpredictable ocean counted for even less. These would have no trouble in swallowing an unwary ship of whatever size. Freak waves of tremendous height were not unknown.

Eventually a petite lady of indefinite age appeared. Ladies are masters of disguising their years.

In a South African accent she enquired, "What can I do for you?"

At the same time she eyed me up and down and in particular my rucksack. I detected a slight concern cross her face when she had completed this inspection. Had she put me in the category of a poor white recently quitting some godforsaken *dorp* in the Karoo? This is the semi desert region of the interior of the Cape Province. Was I trying to gain a Dick Whittington existence in *Kaapstad*?

I said nervously, doubting a fruitful outcome, "I am about to become a freshman, a new student at the University of Cape Town. I want to lodge at your hotel for an indefinite period. Board and lodging is required for a student of very limited means."

The concern on the receptionist's face, although I suspected she was of higher rank from her demeanour, possibly even the owner, disappeared. It was replaced by a bemused smile. This no doubt was encouraged by my cockney accent. It betrayed me as originally a citizen of no mean city.

Denise Van Hoogstraaten said, "I will allocate you the cheapest room. It is very basic but it might serve your needs. In consequence only a fraction of the average rate will be charged especially as you will be a long-term guest. You will be entitled to full board having your meals with the rest of the guests in the restaurant. This will also be at a specially reduced rate."

All this was music to my ears. Denise had apparently taken a shine to me!

Ms Van Hoogstraaten pressed a button at the side of the desk.

At the same time saying, "Moses will show you to your quarters, the restaurant and bathroom." Almost as an afterthought, as Moses appeared, she added, "I will have to see your passport. You can do this on your return with Moses."

Moses was a tall, lean, coloured man, a person of mixed race as opposed to a pure bred African. To my surprise he led me out of the main building. We walked through the garden. He was leading me "up the garden path." As we walked along and chatted I noticed he had an accent that was not what I would have called southern African.

I asked Moses, "Where are you from?"

This seemed to please him as he proudly announced, "I am from St Helena." I had vaguely heard of this place.

Moses explained, "It is a small island in the middle of the South Atlantic, one thousand miles from the African coast. You have to travel an equal distance to reach Cape Town." I belatedly got a fix on the spot in my mind. Geographical locations have always interested me especially when they are remote. This means to me they have interesting people of whatever race.

Moses added with emphasis, "My island is a British possession and therefore I have a British passport," seemingly a further reason for his pride.

Apparently it was traditional for the younger members of St Helena to seek employment in Cape Town. These were invariably of mixed race. They were no doubt a product of seamen who periodically broke the huge distances across the South Atlantic. The islanders were valued workers in South Africa because of their conscientiousness. They knew Cape Town was their main source of income as jobs on the island were limited and poorly paid.

My room was some distance from the main hotel building. It was a dwelling on its own with no upstairs and no rooms adjoining. It was more in the nature of a gardener's bothy. I suspected it had been used in the past as accommodation for a coloured or black worker. Although there was glass in the window the light from this was partially obscured by substantial iron bars. These were welcome for security in view of the fact that the "room" was isolated. It was in a semi-jungle of subtropical shrubs, tree ferns and palms. Yet it had the distinct ring of a prison cell, an impression reinforced by the massive oak door which creaked on its hinges.

At some time in the distant past the interior walls had been whitewashed in the same hue as the exterior. This embellishment was peeling in several places. It revealed the crumbling masonry beneath, which here and there had flecks of powdery fungi (mildew), an indicator of dampness. The concrete floor was firm. Furnishings as one would have expected in such basic accommodation were in keeping with the room. There was an iron framed bed which seemed to be adequately sprung, a wooden cabinet and chest of drawers. At least these latter wooden items were solid and appeared to have a good deal of life left in them. They were a world apart from the self assembly flat packs which modern DIY enthusiasts knock together.

Moses said sympathetically, "The hotel will provide bed linen if you decide to stay."

I followed Moses back to the main building and into the dining room as well as having a quick look at the bathroom. Moses then accompanied me back to the reception desk with a quizzical look on his face. No doubt wondering whether I liked his tour so much that I decided to stay.

Denise Van Hoogstraaten was not at her post. She probably had more pressing duties behind the scenes. Moses rang the bell and the good lady appeared with a smile on her face.

I said enthusiastically, "I accept your kind offer of an indefinite stay at your hotel."

This broadened her smile and I proffered my passport. This was a dark blue hardback booklet with my London home address and my photograph. Moses seemed to sport an even broader smile, no doubt because he felt a comradeship. We were both citizens of the greatest empire the world had ever seen, on which the sun never set. We were entitled to the protection of her Britannic Majesty.

South Africa, although in the British Commonwealth, did not have citizens that were afforded the same protection as those in British colonies. This was because the country was self governing. It didn't matter what the Nationalist Government of South Africa, made up essentially of Afrikaners, might envisage for the non-whites, as far as Moses was concerned. Moses had the comfort of a British passport, unlike the majority of the South African coloureds. He could fall back on the mercy of her Majesty.

In a slightly bemused way Denise flicked through my passport, studying the immigration stamps. There was a transit stamp for South Africa dated two and a half years previously. There was a similar one for Bechuanaland, and an entry stamp for Rhodesia. Additionally there was an exit stamp for Rhodesia and an entry stamp for Bechuanaland dated barely a month before she inspected them. Then she flipped over the pages again.

Denise said in a concerned voice, "I cannot see any recent entry stamp for South Africa."

At this observation my heart sank. I had no recollection of submitting my passport for inspection to a South African official when I entered the Union.

Denise van Hoogstraaten raised herself to her full height, which did not amount to much. She had an ever increasing concern on her face.

She enquired, "When, where, and how did you enter the Union of South Africa?"

Her voice had changed from a somewhat gentle English-speaking South African accent to an almost extreme Afrikaans one. It was as if by some magic carpet she had transported herself to the Afrikaners' heartland somewhere in the interior of the vast subcontinent. She had spiritually left the more genteel environment of Cape Town.

By way of an excuse for my oversight I said, "I hitchhiked across Southern Rhodesia and Bechuanaland. I entered South Africa near Mafeking. After this I did a grand tour of the Union before arriving in *Kaapstad*."

Her face took on an extra dimension at this revelation so that in addition to concern there was a slight tinge of disbelief.

Then somewhat spluttering over her words she said, "You have missed out a most important ingredient in your *Groote Trek.*"

I felt by using the last two words I had been accepted into the great clan of the *Voortrekkers*. These were the Afrikaner pioneers who had laid the foundation of South Africa. Denise continued, "You should have presented yourself and in particular your passport at the *Zuid Afrikaans* immigration office in Mafeking on entering the Union. As you have not done this you are a *persona non grata!*"

I said, "When I first arrived in southern Africa two and a half years ago crossing international borders was no problem. This was because passengers from the Union Castle mail ship were shepherded through customs and immigration on arrival at Cape Town. There was no problem on the two thousand mile journey on the train across the wide open spaces of the Karoo, and onto the High Veld of Rhodesia. Three international borders were crossed with not the slightest of hitches for the train was essentially a boat train. Most passengers seemed to be from the *Edinburgh Castle* boat bound for Southern Rhodesia. Immigration officers were on the train, walking the corridors and making sure you were kosher and stamping your passport. I was spoon fed as far as passport formalities were concerned."

At this point I paused briefly in my defence of my omission to present my passport on entering the Union. I had private thoughts on what a privileged mode of transport I was talking about to Denise. There was no room for smugglers across borders, whatever their colour. This was a train for whites only.

I continued my defence before Denise, "Hitchhiking across frontiers is problematic. You must be alert to misunderstanding especially when entering a country by the back door. Entering South Africa from Bechuanaland apparently was just that.

Bechuanaland was a country few had heard of. Why should they? It was a poor country that most Europeans just passed through. This was on their way from South Africa to Rhodesia. I failed to register my particulars on the South African border because there was no customs and immigration post that I could see. There was no one to lead me by the hand."

All this by way of excuses was too much for Denise Van Hoogstraaten and heightened Moses amusement. After all nothing ever happened like that in St Helena, at least since Napoleon was imprisoned by the British there. He died of poisoning from chemicals in the wallpaper in the residence where he was under house arrest by the British.

So Denise threw up her hands and said, "You can stay at my hotel provided you sort out your passport within a week."She then presented me with a key to my room. I nodded to Moses who by this time had a broad grin on his face tinged with the suggestion of sympathy.

As I walked out into the sun, which by now was quite low on the horizon, I reflected on my future course of action. I recognised I needed to register at the University before going to see the police about my passport. It was clear it would look much better if I had proof of some commitment to use my time in South Africa fully and productively. Those distant times did not witness the army of young Dick Whittington's from a host of countries that registered on a college course. This was usually to learn English. This was to prolong their stay in the new country, most frequently Britain. The very next day they disappeared into the woodwork. They were soon afterwards working illegally in some unmentionable trade. Hopefully I would not be put in that category. Student registration was two days away so I decided to explore the walk to the University the following day.

Reaching my room I unlocked the door with some difficulty. Most keys and locks have their eccentricities. Then the full import of my decision to put up in this humble hovel dawned upon me. The cave before me made me realise that my room at Sabi was fit for a Prince. Even my ex-RAF nissen hut accommodation near Salisbury, Rhodesia, was almost luxury compared with the cell I now found myself in.

I placed the change of clothes I had carried in my rucksack in the cupboard and chest of drawers with plenty of room to spare.

I decided to decorate the walls with a few cuttings. These I had removed from magazines and newspapers during my time in Africa. Foremost among these was my pin-up Kim Novak, an American film actress all the rage at the time. She had also adorned the wall of my Rhodesian room. Looking back over the years I think of her picture as a good omen, for she had a Czechoslovak surname. Years later I was to marry a Slovak girl in that eastern European country decades before the fall of the Iron Curtain.

The other foremost picture on the wall was of a man who was far from the public eye and unknown to me. He was Fred Roast, a stevedore on one of the quays that lined the innumerable docks to which the merchant ships would tie up. They were from the far-flung corners of Empire, in the Pool of London, alas all gone. Somehow his picture appealed to me possibly because my great grandfather and grandfather were associated with docks and the open sea respectively.

On glancing at my watch I saw that seven o'clock was almost upon me and it was time to savour the evening meal. Moses had earlier indicated the table I should sit at, one that overlooked the garden. It was a self service affair in contrast to being spoilt in the Sabi mess by the cook and serving house boys. The food was more than adequate, a mixture of British, Continental and South African dishes.

I had barely sat down when I was joined by a rather continental looking fellow of about thirty, average height and build. He had a cravat tucked into the top of a shirt, enveloped with a navy blue blazer. He introduced himself as Ivan Goddard. Ivan was followed by a tall slim lady well into her thirties with a continental accent. Natty was modestly dressed in a jacket and slacks. It was obvious as time went on that Ivan and Natty were an item. At first I felt out of place in this situation, a kind of Cape gooseberry. A term apparently used in English to describe a person who tags himself on to an enamoured couple. The term suggests he or she is not welcome by them. They try to shake him or her off at the earliest opportunity!

However, it was not like that at all possibly because Ivan and Natty were not as enamoured as I thought. We got on so well that we went on excursions together. This was around the natural environment surrounding Cape Town, be it the mountains or the glorious beaches. We were often joined by other young guests from the hotel whenever a weekend or national holiday allowed. I was not aware of the term Cape gooseberry until just before I wrote these lines. This was when looking for an unrelated word in the dictionary. Never could a term be more appropriate. The district around Cape Town was, and still is, referred to as the Cape.

The author and Ivan (L to R) on a Cape Town beach.
Photo taken by Natty, Ivan's girlfriend, 1958.

We chatted over our main meal followed by caramel sweet which must have been a great favourite of the cook and fortunately of mine. It was served up frequently.

Ivan said, "I am a postgraduate student pursuing a Master of Science degree in geology at the University."

He gained that higher degree a few months later when he was awarded the highest grade possible. His degree involved a dissertation on geological mapping of a part of the Cape hitherto unmapped in detail. Many years later I gained a Master of Science degree in environmental science from London University. This involved a dissertation as well as examinations by dint of evening class study while teaching in an inner London comprehensive school.

Ivan's enthusiasm for rocks encouraged me to take geology as one of my subjects at Cape Town University. Additionally I was stimulated by the emphasis on mining for precious metals and diamonds in southern Africa at that time.

Natty, Ivan's frequent companion, was from the Netherlands and therefore a speaker of high Dutch as opposed to Afrikaans, a derivative of Dutch. She was a gentle lady, significantly taller than Ivan.

I remember her saying, "Many Dutch people regard the South African version of their language with amusement because of its simplification of Dutch."

My reply was haughty, "Afrikaans I have read, uses words imported from the varied people of South Africa, European and native African. English is also a mongrel language made up of words borrowed from a host of countries."

I found this comparison interesting for it reflected on the effect on the language of a people long isolated from the mother country, Holland. The Afrikaners were surrounded and hugely outnumbered by black people who had vastly different languages and cultures. The Africans were thousands of years behind the Afrikaners at the time of their settlement of South Africa four hundred years earlier. In my mind I welcomed that the Afrikaans language was different to Dutch.

It emphasised the dynamic evolution of speech. Afrikaners were as much a product of Africa as of Europe. Some observers regard them as the "white tribe of Africa".

I had a restless night in my isolated room which made me feel I was some kind of leper.

University most beautiful

In the morning after a breakfast of bacon and eggs I set out on foot to explore the route to the University.

Ivan told me, "It's only a mile away."

The suburban road led towards Devil's Peak, a mountain over three thousand feet high, comparable to the highest mountains in England. On the lower slopes of this mountain I understood the University stood. The road soon petered out, and I was free of palatial residences some of which had been turned into hotels similar to mine.

I defy anyone to find a better site than that of the
University of Cape Town on Devil's Peak, 1958.

Devil's Peak and Table Mountain, left to right respectively.

By way of contrast, I entered a pine wood, composed of a species associated with the Mediterranean region of Europe. The trees were fairly uniform in age, perhaps approaching one hundred years. I followed a steepening path which wended its way northwards through these magnificent trees which gave the air a fragrance associated with the resin of conifers.

The pine wood was a plantation. Such woods can be oppressive, as I found some Forestry Commission plantations in Britain can be if they are too closely planted. But the wood that I picked my way through had an airy consistency. Shafts of light broke easily through the canopy.

The plantation had been managed, thinned. Trees felled here and there over the years. The ones that remained were not stunted by the proximity of their fellows. Theirs was a competitive struggle to capture the maximum amount of light and nutrients. The pines had room to make their individual way perhaps displaying quirks of growth due to eccentricity in the micro environment. This wood had a slope which was steeper than a neighbouring one, a rocky spot, a patch of soil that had more nutrients than an adjacent one.

In this magical wood squirrels scampered through the branches. Like the pine they were exotic to these parts, foreign mammals, a hemisphere away from their native environment. The Europeans brought them to the Cape to remind them of home.

I emerged from this spiritually uplifting place into a rose garden. Nothing could be more contrasted. I threaded my way past the thorns that assailed me on either side, but compensated by fragrant blossoms of all hues. They were a bit, I thought, like women. They have the scent and colour but woe betide you if you let them down!

I stepped clear of the rose garden and could see in the distance buildings with a classical, well weathered look. They were arranged magnificently on terraces cut into the lower slope of Devil's Peak. The latter gave the impression of a mountain standing alone. It was really joined to its broader, loftier neighbour, Table Mountain, which was out of sight due to its different alignment. There was no doubt I was confronted by the University of Cape Town. I had seen its iconic picture in the prospectus I received by post in Rhodesia.

The components of University of Cape Town
laid-out on terraces, 1958.

Overwhelmed by the beauty of the scene I was brought to my senses by the swish of a vehicle just in front of me. This broad highway was Rhodes Drive. It led to the world-famous Kirstenbosch Gardens, some three miles away. These were, and are, the national botanical gardens of international fame. They concentrate on the plants of South Africa, and in particular the *fynbos* of the Cape. Further on, some five miles away, was the equally famous beach of Muizenberg lapped by the waters of the South Atlantic.

I had truly chosen an incomparable place to start my university studies, a belief which has not been shaken by time.

On crossing the road I came to extensive playing fields with rugby goals. This was the game of the University and indeed South Africa. However, football has gained in popularity particularly among the blacks. A high wall separated the rugby field from the terraces above it. On these terraces the different components of the university stood. Access to them was by a long flight of steps through and above the wall.

Reaching the first terrace, immediately beyond the wall, I was greeted by the full panoramic sweep of the University of Cape Town campus. The mellowing buildings were clad with the appealing foliage of creepers. They were reminiscent of ivy, but turned later into glorious colours. The university ranged in successive tiers above me.

I ascended the broad, paved, central walkway lined with pencil cedars, another reminder of the Mediterranean region of Europe where they are native. The walkway ascended steeply through the terraces, splitting the campus into two. Crowning the top of this walkway, reminiscent of a processional road but of much greater inclination and narrowness, was a prominent building. This echoed the proportions and decor of a temple, with its classical lines. This impression was reinforced by columns. I learnt this was the Jameson Hall. The students assembled here for a myriad of functions including balls, examinations, and graduations.

Cape Town University before me, 1958.

Here on the following day I would register as a freshman for the class of 58.

I passed the male and female student halls of residence, Baxter and Fuller Halls, separated by the route I was following. Ascending further I crossed a road which was joined at both ends by slip roads curving around the wings of the campus. They joined Rhodes Drive, which led to the centre of Cape Town in one direction and the ocean in the other. Ranged along the internal campus road, opposite the student halls of residence were the various department buildings grouped into faculties. These were collections of related departments, where students would assemble in lecture theatres.

Not all the wide spectrum of studies could be housed in these buildings, which were composed of the same stone as the central part of the site. The stone was reminiscent of Portland stone. This was a limestone much favoured in Britain for the earlier public buildings. The more recent university buildings housed the newer subjects such as astrophysics, geochemistry

Highest part of walkway to Cape Town University.
Jameson Hall at the top. 1958

and the like. They occupied the back of the campus higher up the mountain. These newer buildings reflected architecturally a more utilitarian view of the world than the nucleus of the University built in the 1920s. Cost was obviously a factor here in the 1950s as well as time which put constraints on architects. More students had to be catered for in the mid 20th century, women were coming to the fore. In spite of this, at the time of my student days at Cape Town University, scholars new and established were overwhelmingly white!

I arrived at the top of the steps, seemingly in the heavens. The view I gained from the entrance to the Jameson Hall, as I turned around, was a great sweep of country. Not just across the genteel suburbs from which I had climbed: Rondebosch, Rosebank, and Newlands, but well beyond, encompassing the Cape Flats. These were some fifteen miles wide over which Cape Town was growing. The African locations, living areas, were particularly located there. Then to the south was the glint of the sea, the South Atlantic. Rearing above the Cape Flats to the east were the Hottentots Holland Mountains.

Turning my eyes from this magnificent panoramic feast I noticed the University's central library, the Jaeger library, adjacent to the Jameson Hall. This was the cornerstone of academic life. I later found it was filled with beautifully bound, matching, coloured, gilt lettered hard covers of erudite journals. Additionally there was an assortment of textbooks of all sizes and colours grouped into their respective subjects. These tomes were overwhelmingly printed in English. Anyone versed in that language, to my mind, had an incredible advantage.

The library was part of the University that the more studious students would use. Those who thought their lecture notes were sufficient for passing examinations were not there.

Students were trickling in and out of the Jaeger Library. This was a few days before the start of the academic year. They seemed older than I expected undergraduates to be and I surmised they were postgraduates. Postgraduates do not confine their studies to the academic year. They ignore the long holidays and even the longest holiday straddling the end of the calendar year and the beginning of the next. Southern hemisphere students like South Africans have a long vacation that incorporates Christmas and New Year. Postgraduates work on their theses through the holidays due to the pressures on them by their supervisors. While undergrads are often living it up on the beach. Perhaps surfing, not the net, for the World Wide Web did not exist. They were surfing the sea waves.

One postgraduate student caught my eye. He was emerging from the library into the sunshine at the top of the steps that I had ascended. This was through the avenue of sleek pointed pencil cedars. He had a beret on his head and he looked like the onion man I had seen in France when cycling through the Champagne. Instead of strings of onions draped around his neck the beret hatted student had a bundle of books under his arm. Even the name Jaeger inscribed on the library had a European continental ring.

Early in 2021 the Jaeger Library was engulfed in a terrible fire which destroyed it and the priceless records it contained. This was apparently due to homeless people camping in the forest surrounding the campus of Cape Town University.

CHAPTER 5

UNIVERSITY REGISTRATION AND POLICE INTERROGATION

A committed student

A day or so after viewing the university had me ascending the staircase to heaven again. This time I was among a crowd of potential first-year students, freshers, about to register. This was done in the Jameson Hall where our subjects were chosen. We jostled each other, girls in pretty summer frocks, and youths mostly in long trousers and buttoned up shirts often, with ties. They were all trying to create a good impression, a contrast from the usual shorts of the summer vacation. The students had two things in common almost without exception. They looked very young, as if they were not old enough to leave school. More significantly they were all white, in a country that was overwhelmingly black!

I was given a registration card after I produced my letter of acceptance from the university. This was the one that followed my call up papers for the Rhodesian Army. This letter saved me from the possibility of bush warfare. If stories from Portuguese East Africa (Mozambique) were to be believed bush warfare was very nasty.

After registration we all swarmed to the other half of the hall. There were trestle tables evenly distributed across the floor of this part of the hall. Each had a prominent notice advertising the discipline on offer. A relevant member of staff was in attendance, around who eager students gathered.

Some students, seemingly the more shifty ones, mostly males, were cruising around the floor. They were eyeing up the girls rather than the subjects on offer. They tagged onto the queues with the prettiest girls, clearly wolves in sheep's clothing. They were willing to sacrifice the subjects they had specialised in at school for as many sexual adventures as they were able to muster. No doubt there were girls in the same category eyeing up the boys. They probably had more serious intent, for college or university is a major recruiting ground for potential husbands.

A tragedy of male and female students in the same academic year is that girls are invariably more mature than boys of the same age. Girls no doubt look with more interest at older boys in the later years of their academic training.

The other unfortunate aspect of higher education is that study can be stressful. This is especially in the more demanding subjects, the sciences and mathematics in particular. Certain non-science subjects can be demanding as well. There is the need to get one's head down into lecture notes and books. This means that a studious student cannot devote as much time to love making as he or she would like.

Some might say because I was significantly older than the majority of the first-year students I might be in with a chance with the ladies. Stacked against this was that I was probably more serious about my studies. Additionally I did not have the moral support of my family. I was a world away from my parents and sisters in London. I suspected that most of my fellow students were local. However, some might be a thousand miles from a parental home, the other side of South Africa or in Rhodesia.

A further consideration was that I was entirely reliant on my own savings acquired from my work in Rhodesia. This financial insecurity worried me. This was outweighed by the wonderfully inspirational project I was about to start and the incredibly beautiful location in which I was to attempt it.

I made my way to the stand which proclaimed "GEOGRAPHY" located on the fringes of the tables that were grouped for the arts. These subjects included history, English literature religious knowledge and the like. But the geography table was also adjacent to the sciences. This juxtaposition of geography with the science trestle tables was appropriate because geography overlaps with a number of subjects. Geography not only embraces the sciences but history, social sciences including economics and sociology.

So I enrolled for geography. This was presided over by a tall, slim, blonde, attractive young lady. She was scarcely older than myself and had a North American accent, the country and region I could not place. That was not to be my first encounter with Kay McGill.

With a smile on her face, as I got up from the table to leave, she said, "You have been wise in choosing my subject." This enigmatic remark somewhat haunted me. She then called me back saying, "You have forgotten to take the timetable of the lectures and in particular the practical." Leggy Miss McGill added, "The practical will be demonstrated by my good self."

This postscript intrigued me for I wondered about it as I searched out the tables for the other subjects I had in mind. What was the nature of this practical with her? I fantasised some time on it so much so that I almost forgot to enrol for any more subjects!

My eye then caught the word "BOTANY" emblazoned on the card prominently displayed over a table. This subject I thought appropriate because plants had been a major feature of my work in Rhodesia, particularly the physiological aspects of them. Foremost in this was the plant's capacity to draw up water through their conducting vessels in the roots and stems to the leaves. By so doing the miracle of photosynthesis could be carried out. Here we have the combination of water and carbon dioxide in the presence of light and heat to make food. Without this most life on Earth would perish. The water conduction part of this process was copied by tensiometers. These were gadgets placed in the soil to measure water content by pressure exerted in drawing water into a porous cup. They were an indication of when to irrigate. I monitored these at an agricultural research station in Rhodesia.

Then there was my work on the poisoning elements, the heavy metals, which would disrupt photosynthesis and kill the plant. So botany was added to geography on my timetable.

CHEMISTRY caught my eye among the sea of titles. These were seemingly jostling each other for supremacy on the ends of pedestals placed in the centre of each subject table. I could hardly reject the subject that excited me for so long and was part of my work as a laboratory technician. This was a subject stemming from the age of witches, wizards and alchemists. They longed to change the base metals into gold. But there was no need to do that in South Africa. Gold was to be found in plenty here. You only needed to know where to look. The ancient African metallurgists, of what was to become Southern Rhodesia, residing in such places as the fabled city of Great Zimbabwe, knew their chemistry. They were knowledgeable about the melting point of metals, casting and amalgams (combining different metals). So I was in good company by opting for this science.

On that note how could I turn my back on GEOLOGY? That subject's table was a few steps away. This subject overlapped considerably with geography. Even beyond the study of the elements of geography: climatology, biogeography, hydrology, human population distribution; geology was the guts of it all. The rocks, determined where people lived. They were the background to regional and economic geography. Rocks: coalfields, oil fields, iron ore deposits and of course gold fields influenced where people plied their trade.

There was an additional reason for taking geology. Might I by knowing something about geology stumble in my wanderings upon untold wealth? I might discover a pipe of diamonds and a metallic glint that was not fool's gold!

What clinched the subject for me was that none other than the charismatic Professor of Geology, Dr Hickson had deigned to grace the recruiting table. He was a PhD Cantab, a Cambridge man. Prof Hickson was not a provincial academic but a man of the world. He was a South African who obtained entrance to England's hallowed halls.

Rhodes scholars were promising students, often postgraduates from the English-speaking world, who were financed in their studies by an endowment of Cecil John Rhodes. By such means aspiring Commonwealth and American students were enabled to study at Oxford University. This was facilitated by Rhodes. He had accumulated a fabulous fortune by his dealings in the development of the gold and diamond fields of South Africa. His wealth also enabled the building of Cape Town University on his estate at Groote Schuur where he lived. Rhodes had a hand in forming the DeBeers diamond mining company, "diamonds are forever," as the advert goes. My association with that company was just around the corner.

Rhodes' education at Oxford was interrupted by frequent journeys to southern Africa to indulge his interests there. Eventually he got his degree.

I left the Jameson Hall clutching my registration card and a very full time table. I wondered how I would find the time to seek out a popsy (a girl).

Police interrogation

I had accommodation at the Devonshire Hill Hotel and a student place at Cape Town University. Armed with these facts I felt more secure to face the *Zuid Afrikaans* police. This was for entering their country by the back door, or more precisely not presenting my passport at the relevant office.

What did the Bushman do when they crossed state frontiers? The Kalahari Desert and its arid fringes overlapped with at least three countries. They were nomads, following the wild animals across the parched veld. The Bushmen and game was no respecter of political boundaries. They followed the rains that would create a new flush of grass bringing the Bush Veld alive again. It thereby resounded to the croak of amphibians, the hiss of snakes and the calls of a myriad of insects and birds.

Political boundaries were the invention of white men created so that they could stake a claim to the natural riches within them. They hoped that the land they encompassed would outdo the productivity of their neighbours.

I liked to think I was partly nomadic for sturdy hitchhikers with my behaviour and outlook can make serendipitous discoveries. Geographers, scientists and I had aspirations in that direction. However, it was some years before I could fulfil the possibility of becoming a professional myself. People in those fields I believe have the element of serendipity in their character. I was to confront the "Bureau of Home Security," or some such name. Would the hard-nosed officials of such an organisation listen to this rambling philosophy?

I had to be contrite, invest myself with stupidity on this major oversight of not recognising the most elementary formality of international travel. This was the presentation of a passport at an international frontier.

How would I get in contact with Customs and Immigration? This was the least threatening title I could imagine. I had to throw myself on their mercy. I thought of going to the student office of the University in Lovers Walk to get advice on extricating myself from being an illegal immigrant.

I hailed a passing student, "Could you please direct me to the students' office."

"Don't bother. There is a great queue of students there." I imagined they had a heavy load of problems to sort out.

The nearest police station would have been the most obvious first port of call as I had all the documents on me to make an application for entry into South Africa. But I was not just requesting permission to enter South Africa. I had been in the country a few days already. I wanted to stay in the country indefinitely!

I had a gut feeling about police generally, throughout the world, including the UK, but in particular the South African police. They were practical men not interested in a complex and convoluted story. Everything had to be reduced to its basics so that a quick decision could be made. Whether it was the right one or not was immaterial. The police had decided. It looked good if they had a clear up rate of one hundred percent. No doubt they were vying with other police stations regarding the number of crimes they had solved.

Seeking the mercy of the duty officer behind the desk of the local police station did not seem to be the right course of action. I imagined being confronted by a large picture of some overweight, fierce Afrikaner, hero, politician or otherwise, staring at me from the wall behind the officer. No, I had to find the Customs and Immigration Office. There I hoped to present myself to some more discerning civil servants rather than the rough diamonds of the police station.

The Afrikaners had a resentment of the English-speaking whites and who could blame them? The British had taken their promised land away from them. However, the union of the old Boer republics and the English-speaking provinces had come together in 1910 in the Union of South Africa. This gave the Afrikaners an opportunity to climb to the top of the administration of the country. Their numbers decided the outcome of the ballot box. They outnumbered the English speaking whites. This meant that the Civil Service was dominated by Afrikaners. By going to the Customs and Immigration Office I was likely to be up against a similar frame of mind as if I reported to a police station!

These were my thoughts for what they were worth! But I had one trump card which I was not aware of!

I decided the best course of action was to go direct to the immigration authority. But where would I find such a building.

It was hardly likely that the man in the street would know of such an office? I could of course thumb through the telephone directory or the equivalent of "Yellow Pages" for Cape Town. The latter publication lists the telephone numbers and location of businesses, local and central government establishments in Britain today. Internet Google was more than four decades away.

Meanwhile I was soaking up the sun and the incredible panorama that had unfolded before me. This was as I descended the first steps below the Jameson Hall. Then the penny dropped, or the equivalent in South African currency at that time. I could retrace the few steps above me and visit the Jaeger Library opposite the Jameson Hall. There I could get one of the librarians to look up the phone number and location of the immigration office in Cape Town.

So I looked around the reference section of the Jaeger library for a member of staff. This was preferably the prettiest female that I could find. My technique in doing this was to pose as a great ignoramus. This in fact might have been the case. However that begged a question. Why was I a student at one of the best universities on the African continent, or indeed in the southern hemisphere if I was an ignoramus? Putting on my most helpless pose I spoke to a sexy looking female librarian, full bosomed and wide hipped.

"Excuse me miss could you provide me with the telephone number and address of the immigration department in Cape Town?"

Not only did my ignorance arouse curiosity but also the nature of my question, the formidable reputation of the institution that I sort. However, the librarian no doubt noted from my British accent perhaps tinged with a Rhodesian brogue that I was not from the local parts. This impression of being a foreigner was undoubtedly reinforced by the unfamiliar London technical college blazer I sported. It was embellished with a crest that denoted the college was located in the ancient county of Middlesex. It is now swallowed up by the administrative area of Greater London.

Felicity beamed with a slight tinge of puzzlement, "Here are the details you required. The Immigration Department is located in the heart of the city near to Adderley Street, the main thoroughfare of Cape Town."

Captivated by her beauty I replied stuttering, "I had better ring them up first as I do not want to be caught up in a queue of people trying to speak to an official."

But had I missed an opportunity of asking delightful Felicity for a date?

So I made an appointment by phone to have an interview with the Immigration Department the next day.

A rather gruff Afrikaner answered, "Bring all relevant documentation, most particularly your passport, university enrolment card and letter from the hotel where you are staying."

I decided to bring additional documents. These included letters offering me the post not only in the Roads Department but the Rhodesian Federal Government's Ministry of Agriculture. This I felt would prove my commitment to southern Africa.

The next day I got the train from Rondebosch to the centre of Cape Town, alighting near Adderley Street. I found the immigration building on a side street.

With some trepidation I told the reception desk, "I have an interview with the 'Homeland Security' officers."

I was directed to an office on the second floor. Although five minutes early, I knocked on the door. I was admitted by a stern Teutonic looking woman in her late thirties. She was tightly buttoned up to the upper neck. Her attire did not allow any man to guess what lay beneath.

In a thick Afrikaans accent she told me, "Take a seat."

This was located in front of three individuals sat behind a table. They were burly looking men in their forties in plain clothes but had a military bearing. They had the characteristic

The main street of Cape Town, Adderley Street, 1958.

tan of South Africans who were not shy to disport themselves under the sun in their spare time.

The lady quickly joined them after she had closed the door. I found the whole atmosphere unsettling, particularly as not a flicker of emotion lighted their faces. Not that one would expect this as they were not interviewing me for a job. On the contrary they were no doubt determining whether I should be sanctioned in some way, possibly even ending up in one of their notorious jails. My emaciated body might be thrown out to the proverbial hyenas at the end of my prison sentence. Wolves were not found in South Africa, not the wild animal kind.

A man in the centre of the row, larger than the others, started the interrogation.

"Why did you come to South Africa and by what means?" He added with emphasis, "Why is there no record of you entering the country?"

This was uttered in the usual unsettling intonation of the English Language by one whose home language is Afrikaans.

I prefaced my answer in a quiet, measured, polite greeting in Afrikaans, which I had learnt from Jock, my Afrikaner mess mate at the Sabi Station. This was reinforced by an occasional dip into a lightweight book on Afrikaans. The impact of this attempt at the language of their homes, although it amounted to barely half a dozen words, was electric! Their faces, without exception creased into a slight smile. I had broken the ice, before I had begun. I considered my skills in diplomacy were poor. However, one thing I had discovered was that even the utterance of a word or two in the language of a foreign host is helpful. It is more than appreciated and can be the difference between hostility and acceptance.

I faced the panel of interrogating immigration officers. That is what I hoped they were, rather than plain clothes police. I described my reason for coming to South Africa. I left out the call-up papers I had received from the Rhodesian army. My means of transport was described from the Sabi Valley to Cape Town. More to the point I outlined the route I took across Bechuanaland.

I explained, "I mistakenly missed out the South African entry formalities from Bechuanaland into the Transvaal." I emphasised, "This was because it apparently did not take place at the border."

At the same time I offered my supporting documents, and in particular my passport.

One of the officers said, "You should have taken your passport to the immigration office in Mafeking."

This town I remembered was some twenty miles further on in South Africa.

I explained, "I first arrived in Africa, by liner at Cape Town. I travelled by train through the Cape Province, Bechuanaland and finally to Salisbury, Southern Rhodesia. This train journey was of enormous length and time, two thousand miles and three days respectively. Although it was one of the great railway journeys of the world it was very straightforward as regards immigration formalities. This was because I used conventional public transport."

This must have been clear from the rubber stamps in my passport I had obtained two and a half years earlier. The officers examined these closely.

I added, "The journey I have just completed was in a different category. I used my own initiative, chose my own route, and commandeered unregulated transport by hitchhiking."

At this point the plainclothes interrogators paused and looked at me. They were probably allowing themselves time to take in the full import of what I was saying and to formulate their next question.

Then as if voicing the trump card in my pack, I appealed to their pride in their Afrikaner culture. I reminded them in a trembling voice, "The Boers on their *Groot Trek* across the unknown interior veld of *Zuid Afrika* did not have passports. They were masters of their own destiny. They did not recognise boundaries which were the invention of the British, the *Roineks*."

I did not feel I could go as far as to say that Africans did not recognise lines drawn by Europeans on the map of Africa. Such national boundaries were highly inconvenient to native people not only in Africa but across the world. The Shona people of eastern Rhodesia among whom I had lived while working in the Sabi Valley found their tribe divided by a frontier. This was between Southern Rhodesia and Mozambique. It was a creation of the British and the Portuguese respectively.

Afrikaners would have no sympathy with the blacks having their tribal areas dismembered in this way in the 19th century. This was rather like farmers in Britain having their farms cut in two by motorways in the second half of the 20th century. Motorists would not have a sympathetic thought about that. Anyway to compare the situation of the Afrikaners with that of the blacks would be a gross insult to both parties.

The officers audibly inhaled their breath when I implied that my hitchhike across southern Africa was a kind of copy of the Boers' trek one hundred years previously.

I hastened to add in case it was realised that I was being too presumptuous, "My journey was done in the spirit of the *Great Trek.*"

No way could I suggest that my difficulties were anything to compare with the sacrifice of the Boer pioneers. Nothing could compare to their struggle to carve a South African nation out of the veld.

It occurred to me that partially I was escaping the persecution of the Rhodesian Army. The Boers were fleeing the interference of the British in the Cape. No way could I make the point that I was escaping military call up. It would sound unpatriotic and cowardly!

Another trump card I realised I had in impressing the officers was that I was intending to educate myself in one of South Africa's premier universities. True, it was not the traditional Afrikaans speaking University of Stellenbosch only thirty miles from Cape Town. This was one of the two universities of South Africa's earliest settled region. The point I was making was it was not just the quality of the educational institution I was about to enter. The fact was it was a South African one in the city where I was being interrogated. I was trying to flatter the officers.

I said, "I have come all the way from London to settle in South Africa no matter how indirectly. Also I am aiming to be educated at a South African University."

However, as I found out later, many of the Cape Town University lecturers and professors were from outside of South Africa including Britain and America. Universities like to recruit the best they can, from wherever, at least the English speaking South African ones.

I continued my appeal to stay in South Africa, "I had partaken of the work ethic of southern Africa by working in Rhodesia. That country is regarded by many as an extension of South Africa because of its similar life style and environment. Indeed I had rubbed shoulders with South Africans who had gone to work and live in Southern Rhodesia. "

So I rested my case and stared the officers in the eyes at its conclusion. There was a pause and all the officers' faces creased into a smile nodding at each other. The buttoned up lady even undid her top button and with a flourish stamped my passport and handed it back to me. Then they all stood up and I followed. Shaking me by the hand they wished me good luck in my studies!

My first date in Cape Town

In the few days I had before starting lectures at the University I tried to familiarise myself with Cape Town and its immediate surroundings. This was possible by the suburban train. Rondebosch Station was only a short walk from the Devonshire Hill Hotel. There were also buses. Hitchhiking was not appropriate in a large city.

I was anxious to get as near to the sea as possible and especially the beach. I had wandered along the glorious sands of Natal and the Eastern Cape Province on my hitchhike trip from the Rhodesian Sabi Valley to Cape Town. However, these were but fleeting encounters in view of my need to get settled down in the vicinity of the University as soon as possible.

The promenade at Sea Point was one of my earliest attempts to renew acquaintance with the seaside near Cape Town. This was barely five miles from Rondebosch and was particularly rewarding for the sights and sounds of the sea. The openness, afforded by extensive lawns studded with palm trees, formed a buffer between the promenade and the highly regarded residences behind. Beyond this rose the awesome uplands of Cape Town. Further away could be seen a range of splendid heights known as the Twelve Apostles. These were so called because the line of their rocky ramparts was cleft by ravines, which split the rock face into twelve prominent broad columns.

They gave the area distinctiveness reminiscent of the Mediterranean's north coast.

Two great prominences reared their steep slopes just beyond the sought-after suburb of Sea Point. These hills were known as Signal Hill and Lion's Head.

There was an open air swimming pool at Sea Point due to the rocky nature of the coast which did not encourage swimming in the sea. I struck up an acquaintance with a popsy there, while disporting ourselves on the grass after a swim. Jane was a pleasant girl, a brunette, and beginning to put on weight. I believe some five years older than me and slightly taller. Those were the days of comparative modesty in dress at least in South Africa. Jane had a swimming costume that only left her legs arms and top of her neck exposed. Most females at that time, except teenagers, dressed in such bathing costumes. The teenagers strangely did not whet my appetite in sporting bikinis as I found when passing through Durban just before arriving in Cape Town. Maybe the more a female covers herself up leaves more to the imagination!

The author and popsie. Sea Point open
air swimming pool, Cape Town, 1958.

I took Jane to the bioscope, a South African term for a cinema. Apparently this word was used in Britain many years previously. This is an example of how words in the "colonies" lagged behind the metropolitan countries, those with colonies. But southern Africa, at that time, had much that reflected American material values. Britain had not caught up yet in that respect. Southern Africa, even in the late 50s, was a strange mixture of early decorum and modern trends. This was a pleasant mixture of customs harping back to pre Second World War days and attempts to enter mid-20th century consumerism.

The film Jane and I saw at the bioscope was supposed to be romantic. However, it was swamped by an incredibly Irish folksy background. It kept harping back to a peasant economy accompanied by Gaelic songs, fiddles and pipes. Somehow it overdid the folksiness that I appreciated up to a point. Anyway I had the good company of Jane, apparently a South African born and bred.

Jane said, "Would you like to come in for coffee?"

Her bedsit was in an ageing block of flats somewhere in a part of Cape Town not as desirable as Sea Point. Nevertheless it was a white's only area. Cape Town was no exception to the policy of apartheid (separateness) between the whites and blacks in South Africa, or indeed in Rhodesia. Jane's flat was sparsely furnished, which was not surprising considering its incredibly small area. There was room for a bed but little else although I did notice a small cooking range in the corner of the room. I assumed the bathroom was some way down the corridor shared by other residents.

Jane invited me to sit down.

She bowled me over by saying, "We will have to sit on the bed I have no coach."

In such situations it is reasonable to suppose that young people of eligible age of the opposite sex would engage in something more intimate than chat. But although Jane was a good companion I did not feel any more. It seemed that it was déjà vu. Similar circumstances surrounded my brief encounter with the nurse from Marandellas, Rhodesia. Unfortunately it is not often possible to have an indefinite platonic companionship with a woman. They inevitably want more.

CHAPTER 6

A FRESHMAN EMBARKS ON HIS STUDIES

Student days begin

The day dawned when I was to receive my first lecture. My timetable was full. I had committed myself to lectures and practicals in four subjects, geography, botany, geology and chemistry. I wondered whether I was being too ambitious.

I made my way towards the geography department of Cape Town University, which was helped by a map I got at registration. If I got lost it was no good taking geography! Pushing my way through a crowd of excited students, I realised they were a mixture of academic years. This melee was highlighted by the interest of the older male students in the female freshers, which was clearly enjoyed by the girls. I glanced with interest at this throng, enlivened by the colourful dresses of the young ladies, for it was late summer in the southern hemisphere. I had to push myself through the crowd.

I said to a couple, "Excuse me but I have got to get to a lecture."

At which a flashy looking student said, "So do we, but first things first."

Passing the students' hall of residence I approached the geography lecture room. This was located in a building which reflected the same appealing architecture as the majority of the campus. This used a pleasing composition of seemingly Portland stone. The limestone mellowed to a light brown cream. The University was barely forty years old, at least at the Devil's Peak site. However, its origins went back to the 19th century in central Cape Town.

Geography, a vibrant mongrel

Choosing a bench in the lecture room that was not too crowded, I was then joined by a group of females. They were flushed with the anticipation of entering a world in which they were treated as adults.

I said to the girl nearest to me, who seemed more excited than the rest, "Would you mind telling your friends to move up? I'm about to fall off the end of the bench." At this they all started giggling. Some lifted their dresses as they slid along the bench.

"Ouch" said one, "I've got a splinter in my bottom." At which they all exploded into laughter.

The air was thick with an assortment of scents. These were no doubt generously daubed all over the girl's bodies. This was supplemented with powder and lipstick, in the other appropriate parts of their anatomy. Shy glances were exchanged with the benches of male students. No doubt they were sticking together with their mates from the local high schools.

But there were others who seemed somewhat out of place. They shared the common denominator of age and colour of skin, white. This group was likely to be from the more distant parts of the Union, including Johannesburg, some one thousand miles away. Perhaps there was even a sprinkling from the British colonies of Africa. Nyasaland, Northern Rhodesia, Tanganyika, Kenya, and of course Southern Rhodesia had significant white communities.

No doubt there was good reason for these distant white communities sending their sons and daughters to the University of Cape Town. Such white groups were increasingly under siege from their black brethren. This applied to the more militant minority of the blacks. At that time this was not felt by the whites in Southern Rhodesia. However, the authorities there were no doubt aware of distant rumblings of "native war drums." After all why was I needed in the Rhodesian Army other than to defend the interests of the whites?

It was likely that by sending their youth to Cape Town the youngsters from territories beyond South Africa could report back to their parents. This was like a report on the state of the Union. This category of students was maintaining a toehold, the thin end of a wedge, in South Africa. Perhaps this would make it easier for their communities in east and central Africa to settle in the Union should the need arise. South Africa was considered throughout Africa as a bastion of white supremacy. It was thought that it would be a long time before this changed, if ever!

The students sitting on the bench waiting for the geography lecturer to appear had to find companions, perhaps soul mates.

It should be remembered that these times were forty years before the appearance of mobile phones. Landline phones invariably involved an anxious queue of youngsters in the corridors of the University halls of residence. Even phoning from the Devonshire Hill Hotel, my digs, involved similar inconvenience. That did not bother me because I never phoned home due to the expense!

A tall, slim, fiftyish, rather pale faced man, surprising as South Africa was a sunny place, entered the lecture room, clutching some papers. The excited crowd quietened down. The man before us was none other than the head of geography Professor Albright.

I heard one girl whisper to her friend, "He looks sickly, about to give up the ghost!"

The University prospectus was sent to me while I was at Sabi, Rhodesia. I noted Prof. Albright did not have a higher degree. No doubt his London University BSc degree was of the highest order. Today a University lecturer is required to have a PhD, Doctor of Philosophy degree. This is in a degree gained by at least three years of full-time research.

I had experience as a part time student and simultaneously as a technician at London University some years after my Cape Town studies. There some lecturers were working part-time towards their PhDs. They were teaching university students while they were working on their theses.

The Cape Town Professor outlined the course in geography. This made it clear it was a mongrel subject borrowing knowledge from a number of other subjects.

We retired to an adjacent much more spacious room. Later experience taught me this was a drawing office. There were tables on which large sheets of parchment paper were laid out. Tracing tables, set squares, pencils, rubbers, all the tools needed by a cartographic draughtsman were there.

A large, stout, rather serious man in his forties, dressed in a dark suit entered the room.

In a South African accent he made it clear, "Proficiency in cartographic drawing is an important skill. This is a necessity to an aspiring geographer!

He was joined by the young lady who I had met earlier at my registration. She introduced herself as the demonstrator in a rather appealing American accent which I later discovered was Canadian.

Kay McGill announced, "I will be moving among you helping you with your drawing exercises." Now I knew what she meant when she said at my enrolment, "You will be having practicals with me."

The first piece of work involved plotting the distribution of the population of South Africa by means of dots. Each dot represented five thousand people, as I recall. These needed to be placed in the correct position on an outline map of the Union. This was done in relation to the census districts. We had been given a list of the population of the census districts and their location prior to the exercise. The dots therefore had to be confined to the area of the census district to which they referred, but evenly dispersed. Often the district was so small that the dots overlapped creating dark smudges on the map, clearly densely populated areas. Where towns and cities occurred and a mass of overlapping dots were inappropriate larger "dots" were used. These circles had diameters proportional to say 50,000, 100,000, 250,000, and 500,000 people. Any excess population over these values were shown by smaller circles.

I have described this exercise in some detail because human population and its distribution are fundamental in explaining the pressures on resources and the environment. This is the greatest problem of any age and is a cornerstone of geography.

On my completed map I noticed that high population density was not confined to the big cities, like Johannesburg and Cape Town. They occurred in some rural areas as well.

I said to Miss Kay McGill, the demonstrator, as she looked at my map, "I hitchhiked through Natal and the adjacent part of Cape Province. This was on my way to this university from Rhodesia. Here African villages (kraals) were close together in the Zulu and Xhosa areas. This is shown on the map as high population density."

Kay beamed, "That is a very good observation Mr Hardy." I felt a tingle in my loins! She remembered my name.

The exercise was completed without too much trouble. What I found particularly testing was the lettering. My hand writing had deteriorated over the years, even at that distant time, in spite of being in my early twenties. In the first year of my private secondary school emphasis was on copy plate writing. Our lettering was based on an illustrated handwriting book. Here the direction of the pen was indicated when writing the components of a letter of a word. This I felt was more appropriate in the junior school. A Miss Wolf instructed us in our lettering exercises, an elderly, full of figure lady.

She repeatedly reminded us, "You are not very bright. Make sure your lettering is right."

I opted later in my private secondary school to go into the "grammar" rather than the commercial half of the school. As a result I ceased to be trained for sitting on a high stool scribing a book keeper's ledger in copy plate writing. Because of this my lettering of the population density of South Africa in my first cartographic exercise at Cape Town University was a bit of a flop. By dint of trying to raise my grades in cartographic exercises my handwriting improved. This was long before computer generated lettering existed.

A particular exercise I enjoyed because it had a strong association with the distribution of natural vegetation was producing a world map of climates. This was based on the Koppen classification. Here we go again! The Germans were giving their names to developments in science in which they had a strong hand!

We were given an outline map of the world with selected place names which had long-term climatic data. No doubt obtained from meteorological stations like the one I supervised at Sabi, Rhodesia. I was given a list of these places with their average annual and seasonal climatic data, particularly temperature and rainfall. This was for a period of many years. The name of the climatic region to which they belonged was given. The data was used to draw lines on the map enclosing climatic areas which could be distinguished from their neighbours by critical climatic values. An important feature was the number of months in the year that had average temperatures above or below a certain value and similarly for rainfall.

Where the winters were wet and mild and the summers hot and virtually rainless highlighted the Mediterranean climate. This was named after the area around the Mediterranean Sea in Europe which has this climate. But this was not the only area in the world that had this idyllic weather. The region encompassing Cape Town and surroundings fell into this category. The Central Valleys of California and Chile, and the southern extremities of Australia also had Mediterranean climates. They were and are regions of popular wines.

Such areas are characterised by similar vegetation types with shrubby plants, rather like heathland, with heather like plants. These have reduced leaves, often waxy in order to conserve water loss in the long dry summer. Such vegetation often had local names like the maquis around the Mediterranean Sea, fynbos close to Cape Town, and the chaparral in California. Mediterranean climatic areas are characterised by a vast array of different plant species including orchids.

A particular feature of the cartographic exercises at Cape Town was the number of North American landscape features we had to draw from map spot heights. From these seemingly random locations, where surveyors had determined heights, we interpolated the course of the contours. Coastal features of the east coast of the United States, including Cape Cod, were emphasised. To add to the American flavour of the course we used American university geography text books, some of which were superb.

I asked Kay when she looked at my cartographic exercise, "Why are there so many American examples in the geography course?"

"It is because the department has a lot of material: maps, photographs, etc, of American geographical features."

This seemed to me a circular argument, but I did not want to challenge her.

I put these American examples down to the influence of leggy Miss McGill. I assumed she was a graduate of a Canadian university, possibly even the famous McGill University, Montréal. I suspected that some of the more senior staff might have had part of their training in America.

There was one particular Canadian geographical feature that was topical at that time. This was the construction of the St Lawrence Seaway, completed in the following year to my studies with Miss McGill. This canal system enabled ocean going ships to reach the heart of North America via the Great Lakes from the Atlantic Ocean.

The overseer of the cartographic student drawing office was the large, dour, South African, Mr Villiers, of indeterminate Afrikaans or English-speaking background.

Mr Villiers criticized me when I was discussing one of the cartographic exercises with him.

He said, "You do not use the term Cape Colony instead of Cape Province when talking about the area you are drawing. In political circles this is a major faux pas. The south-west part of South Africa, in which Cape Town occurs, has not been referred to as Cape Colony for many decades. This term stems from the overthrowing of Afrikaner rule at the Cape by the British."

I believe I made this quip deliberately because Mr Villiers was so dour. I suspected Mr Villiers never forgave me for this indiscretion.

Later in the course he suggested, "You are a 'plant', a kind of spy. You must be reporting back to some British educational quango on the standards of teaching in Commonwealth countries!" I was concerned, flattered and amused all at the same time by this outburst.

This is the kind of suspicions generated by individuals who are seen not to be part of the crowd, mavericks. This must go on all over the world! Obviously such individuals have to tread cautiously for fear of being misunderstood. Explorers, geographical and otherwise, and I include scientists in this category, "go where angels fear to tread."

Some time into my studies at Cape Town I got talking to a lecturer, a tall slim chap in his late thirties, with a British accent. Mr Brown had not taught me on any of my courses.

He said, "I am surprised you have come to Cape Town University. This is a very distant place in which to study. To many in Europe it would be regarded remote.

Stung by this remark I said, "I am surprised by your take on our shared magnificent venue. I would have thought you would see there are distinct advantages in you teaching and me studying in this gloriously beautiful part of the world.

Additionally it has a climate to match." Indeed, I believed that the University of Cape Town had, and has, the best campus and setting of any university in the world.

I got the impression that the lecturer who button holed me, Tom Brown, knew something I did not know. Perhaps he knew the Nationalist, Afrikaner government, was putting pressure on the University to conform in some sort of away. It is well know that many universities throughout the world often have a more liberal take on who and how they should educate their students. Indeed they have views on how the country should be run, which is often at variance with their government. I should qualify this by saying that it is more likely that some of the students had these views rather than the University authority.

A university's existence depends on having good relations with the government. Their students can afford to be opinionated because they are transitory. The lecturer, Tom Brown, alerted me very indirectly about the politics and potential politics which could bring instability. In the meantime politics did not seem to affect me. I was going to enjoy all the incredible advantages of being a white student at the Cape of Good Hope. I felt this name, almost the southerly extremity of the African continent, augured well for the future!

My stay in Cape Town was at a time when the University and the city, as well as the natural surroundings had not been excessively developed. This invariably happens everywhere with the huge increase in population as many decades pass. In fact I visited Cape Town for the first time in 2016 after I left that city in early 1959. I found it had changed almost beyond recognition. The population had increased from six hundred thousand to over five million.

Instead of the single carriageway of Rhodes Drive which curved sympathetically just below the university campus there was a motorway with several lanes. Along this vehicles hurtled, unaware of the beauty that had been there sixty years previously.

I said to Sarah, my black taxi driver, a thirty something, voluptuous, pleasant lady, "Could you drop me and my wife at the university?"

Sarah said, "As you can see the university campus is full of parked vehicles. I am unable to stop."

So we had only fleeting views of the fine old buildings now one hundred years old. My taxi driver was from Zimbabwe. Like a number of her compatriots she had fled Zimbabwe. This helped to swell the population of Cape Town. We hired Sarah for four days in order to see the sights of Cape Town, so we got to know her quite well.

Plants, spies they are not

Plants, not the spy variety already referred to, I studied at UCT. Botany was a subject I enjoyed at the Cape. As well as lectures there were the practicals, aided by the demonstrators. The latter were quite friendly, no doubt postgraduate students. I suspected they were completing the write-up of their higher degree theses. They were nothing compared to leggy Miss McGill, the geography demonstrator.

The demonstrators had been through the mill, some presumably recently. They had obtained their first degrees, their Bachelor of Science. However some looked particularly mature, seemingly in their thirties and forties.

A particularly testing practical was the cutting of a very thin section of the stem of a plant, often only a couple of centimetres in diameter. This was done with a cut-throat razor which had to be sharpened by hand. It was moved up and down a strop, a narrow piece of leather. I used to see an uncle of mine do this. As a boy I stayed with him while my father was away in the Second World War.

The botanical "thin" section was placed on a microscope slide, a small transparent piece of glass. A variety of chemicals were added from small dropping bottles, which stained the different tissues in this section a different colour. This allowed them to be distinguished from each other. The problem was the plant tissues often got entangled with small pieces of my skin and flesh where I had clipped the top of my finger. So viewing this mess down the microscope was like a "Spanish village" as they say in Eastern Europe.

Repeating this process till I got a perfectly thin section of the plant species stem was physical and mental torture. I got into a strop. The demonstrator was not one to be disappointed when checking your work.

She said, "You must practice cutting the plant stem until you have mastered the technique. The names of the parts in your drawing of the cross section of the stem must be under each other. They should be in a column down the side of the page."

This section when viewed under the microscope revealed plant tissues. These tissues were collections of similar cells. The tissues differed. They were specialised to carry out different functions, such as conduction of water and sugars. There were tissues with specially thickened cells that reinforced the strength of the stem like steel rods in concrete. Unlike steel they had to bend in the wind. These had to be drawn and labelled in copy plate writing. Again, as in geography I had difficulty in lettering.

Cross sections of plant stems varied for different species, though the basic plan remained the same. Variations were dependent on the habitat from which they came. They might be from a marsh where less rigid support was required because of the buoyancy of water.

On the rocks

Geology was a particularly exciting subject. It involved fieldwork unlike the other subjects I took. This was surprising because geography and botany are concerned with the environment. None other than the Professor of Geology, Head of Department, took us into the field.

Universities in Britain and the Commonwealth used the term professor to designate the head of an academic department. He or she had served with distinction in a University. Some professors were national or even international figures. The majority of lecturers in a British or Commonwealth universities were therefore not professors. No doubt they all aspired to that position. They needed to work through a hierarchy of lecturer, senior lecturer, and reader to reach the lofty position of professor.

I described my viva, an interview where I defended my written thesis for a research degree of London University, to an acquaintance. He was an American who first graduated in the States. I emphasised that a professor from another British university questioned me on my thesis. This was to avoid bias of academic staff towards their own students. There was no room for favouritism.

My acquaintance interjected, "Only a professor!"

It turned out from the conversation with James that all university lecturers in the States are called professors. This is the case no matter how low they are in the hierarchy.

I believe the term professor is even used for staff in academic institutions below university level in some parts of the world.

I said, "None other than the Head of the Faculty of Biological Sciences, the external examiner, led the two-hour interrogation. He was accompanied by internal academic staff, lecturers from the College of London University where I was a part-time student."

My "talk" was put in perspective. Acquaintances, relatives and neighbours are some of the most critical of people regarding my attainments!

The field work in geology took me and the first year students well beyond Cape Town and its immediate surroundings. It was an opportunity to look at the rocks and deduce their formation. This was done not just from their composition of varied minerals. We examined the way in which they had been folded and contorted over eons of time.

Here time, "Had not the vestige of a beginning or end," to paraphrase the words of a pioneer geologist. It afforded an appreciation of the varied landscapes of the Cape on foot. Hitherto it had been from a speeding train when journeying to Rhodesia and a speeding car when leaving it as a hitchhiker. Geology field work enabled me to rub shoulders with fellow students and staff, many of whom seemed very bright indeed.

Studying geology, in my view, transcends any religion. It makes it clear that humans, in spite of the hype, are insignificant. The unimaginable billions of years that the rocks of our planet have witnessed emphasises this conclusion. We have been here five minutes in comparison to the age of the earth. The subject promotes humility.

Geology field trips required the use of coaches and walking over rough terrain in tough clog hoppers. Wind and waterproof attire was needed in the Cape winter, with the occasional need for camping overnight. This was because some sites were distant. They were far away from European settlements, as far as the arid Karoo. Often the geological curiosities were among the magnificent mountains of the Cape. Sometimes there were vineyards on their lower slopes. Hot springs were a special feature where sulphurous compounds were brought to the surface. The water had been heated at depth.

Geology practicals included observing mineral structure by peering down a microscope at thin sections of rock.

I said to the demonstrator, "Thankfully these thin sections of the rocks are provided by the geology department. The student has to cut their own sections in the botany department." She laughed heartily at this remark.

Additionally different species of fossil which characterised the different ages of sedimentary rocks had to be drawn. Sedimentary rocks resulted from the laying down of sediments in water with subsequent drying and compaction.

The author, extreme left, with students on a
UCT geological field trip, South Africa, 1958.

UCT geology students immersed in the rocks.
Professor (Head of Dept) talking to driver. 1958.

UCT geology students trekking through semi-desert
of the Karoo, South Africa, 1958.

UCT geology students on top of an Inselberg
in the Karoo. South Africa, 1958.

"Mind your step!" UCT geology students by a boiling
hot spring. South Africa, 1958.

The alchemy of wizards and witches

Chemistry was an oversubscribed subject. The students seemed
to be jostling each other for space, particularly in the
laboratories. What I found tedious was when we were given
an exercise that involved weighing out a chemical on a delicate
balance. Students were queuing up with some even trying to
jump the queue.

I said to one precocious individual, "Just because you're
bigger than me you don't have to muscle in."

He retorted, "I thought I was on the rugby field where the
slow get outrun."

This experience contrasted with my work in my technician
post at the Sabi Agricultural Research Station in Rhodesia.
There I was the only one to use the fine chemical balance. It
weighed to ten thousandths of a gram. The sensitive weighing
machine was encased in a glass surround to hold back draughts
and dust. It was hived off in an alcove of the laboratory. I
could take my time at weighing at Sabi. There was no one

breathing down my neck wanting to get onto my stool. Clearly I was spoilt at the experiment station. My work was done at a leisurely pace. Hopefully there was no comparison here with a snail. My line manager was on research work in Mormon country, America.

I hold the view that the older you are the more you want your own space. Most school pupils put up with the rough-and-tumble of their peer group, they have to. This I believe follows into the early years of adult life at college. I was used to having my own bench space in all the work I did since leaving school at sixteen. This included the company industrial chemical laboratory in London, the Rhodesian Road Department's laboratory, and the Rhodesian Sabi situation just described. All enabled me to have breathing space, bench space.

I did not like the claustrophobic atmosphere of the University of Cape Town's Chemistry Department. I knew I had a very full timetable and I wanted to concentrate on those subjects in which I was most relaxed. I had gathered a respectful fund of knowledge about chemistry over the years before I entered the university. However, I dropped chemistry at Cape Town! In my subsequent working life I returned to the subject, working at it over some years. It was one of the great interests of my life. However, I was not taught science at school.

CHAPTER 7

CLIMBING TABLE MOUNTAIN AND SPUTNIK RAG

Tennis with Freda

The Devonshire Hill Hotel was a welcome balance to the youthful melee of the University. Ivan, Natty and my good self were joined at our regular hotel restaurant table by a pleasant German lady. She was in her late twenties. Some six years older than me, slightly taller and quite good-looking. Normally I went on local excursions at the weekends with my two regular restaurant friends. These were topped up with the occasional lady from elsewhere in the hotel. A semi permanent foursome was made when Freda joined us.

A favourite spot of ours was the Western Province tennis courts where the great South Africa matches were played. It was only a few hundred yards from the Devonshire Hill Hotel. Adjacent to the hallowed courts was a knockabout tennis court where we could try out what little skill we had in the game.

I have a curious turn of mind, not for gossip, I leave that to those ladies that are so inclined. However, some men have that disposition. I am curious about the way society ticks in a generalised way. This of course is in addition to my curiosity about geography and science.

One of my concerns was how the German people allowed the rise of the Nazi movement. Back in the late fifties of the twentieth century, the time about which I am writing, Nazi atrocities were still fresh in the memory of British people. So I sounded out Freda on this emotive subject.

"Freda, how do you explain the beastliness the Germans meted out to the Jews?"

It was bad enough raising this topic when we were on our own. To broach this subject in the company of Natty and Ivan was to say the least insensitive. In my defence I would say my curiosity got the better of me. I was looking for some personal insight that Freda might have given me on that topic.

Freda reluctantly answered me saying, "Most of the German people did not have a say in the matter. They were intimidated."

Realising the indiscretion of my question I tried to soften it.

I said, "The British are partly to blame as they invented the concentration camp in South Africa during the Boer War."

The British Army raided the farm houses of the Boer men folk and took away their women and children. They herded them into camps. Many of these people died of disease and hunger in the camps. This was done to deny the Boer fighters the support of their families. It was done to turn the battle around in Britain's favour. The Boers for some time had been successfully fighting the British in a hit and run campaign. The British Army eventually prevailed through ever increasing numbers of tommies shipped out from Britain.

I could scarcely expect Freda to give me a definitive answer on the apparently split personality of Germans. Many of them were cultured but at the same time cruel. Young ladies did not want to consider such subjects which could be embarrassing if they were German. This was especially the case when they wanted to relax on the tennis court. I was, and still am, too serious minded for my own good.

Unhappiness among the guests

There were two other personalities at the Devonshire Hill Hotel who intrigued me. One was a slim woman in her thirties of average height with a pronounced South African accent. Stella seemed worn by care which had drained any good looks she might have had. This was reinforced by her modest clothes. Stella was often accompanied by a boy of about seven years of age. She occupied a room on the ground floor of the hotel which opened onto the garden. Here her boy would play.

Stella said to me, "Sadly, Johnny has no playmates at the hotel."

It was obvious, as the months past, that she was a single mother. My eldest daughter, when she settled briefly in South Africa forty years after my African odyssey, found similar problems among her mature South African friends.

The other case in which the Devonshire Hill Hotel helped out was a crippled man in his late seventies. He had an iron on his leg and consequently he had difficulty in walking. Trevor, like Stella had a single room at ground level in the hotel overlooking the garden.

Trevor said to me one day while I walked about the garden, "All my friends and relatives have died. I am the only one left."

My experience of meeting people at the Devonshire Hill Hotel, and indeed outside in Cape Town, was that South Africa had social problems among the whites. These were associated with the lack of connection between people of the opposite sex and the isolation of the elderly. I found the same thing among the bachelors and the aggressive mechanic at Sabi, Rhodesia. In my naivety I believed the rural Africans were happier in their traditional village society. But that was breaking down in the face of the white man's monetary driven life style. It seems the more affluent a country is the more social problems occur. To my mind southern Africa had anticipated Britain's descent into this thorny area.

Ascending the *Tafelberg*

The four of us, Ivan, Natty, Freda and my good self, would explore the surroundings of Cape Town. On the occasion of tackling Table Mountain we were joined by two other young ladies, Gillian and Jackie. They were in their thirties and also from our hotel. Table Mountain loomed above the city. Its precipices appeared to threaten to collapse at any moment and push our idyllic *Kaapstad* into the sea.

So stark were the cliffs of the northern face of Table Mountain that the mountain seemed un- climbable. However, there were concealed *kloofs* (clefts) in its otherwise grim face. Here shrubs and herbs were able to ascend to the heights. They were not able to do this on the cliffs on either side. Plants had no purchase on such a sheer unforgiving natural edifice. Where low shrubs could go a path could also. The imprints of hobnailed boots testified to the stalwarts who ventured to the summit in this way.

Of course there were the more genteel who ascended the mountain by the cable car in a matter of minutes. They crowned their excursion by a reward in the form of a tea room, as I did on one occasion. The fare was expensive.

One of the lower stations on the cable car could be reached by a road which zigzagged up the lower slope. This was a favourite spot for Vesper bikes, lightweight motorbikes which were all the rage with young people at the time.

Our party from the Devonshire Hill Hotel managed to scramble up the steep path in the *kloof*, our light weight rucksacks on our backs. They contained little in the way of extra clothing. Even in winter in Cape Town it could be mild. Additionally our exertions made us hot. This was tempered by the shade cast by the sides of the very narrow valley we were ascending. The fall in temperature with altitude added to the freshness.

Natty said to Ivan, who was leading the climbing party, "Can you slow down? I am exhausted."

Gill nodded assent and said, "We should stop to drink some water."

Table Mountain is three thousand five hundred feet high. This is almost identical with Snowdon, the highest mountain

Hotel friends climbing up Table Mountain, 1958.

in Wales. This can be seen from my youngest daughter's house on a clear day. In both cases these mountains rise close to the sea which makes them appear higher than they really are.

We rested during our exertions, each time affording a more magnificent view than the earlier rest stop. Not only was an ever larger extent of Cape Town revealed but also the incredibly varied environment beyond. We were facing a different direction to the viewpoint afforded by the steps up to the University on the slopes of Devil's Peak. Table Mountain looked south over the centre of the city and the docks beyond. It was subject to the moisture that came in from the clash of the oceans to the south. Here the Cape Peninsula ended and the cold currents of the Atlantic Ocean approached the warmer waters of the Indian Ocean further east.

Our climbing party was lucky to avoid mist, low cloud, which often enveloped the upper reaches of the mountain, given the name of "table cloth." It often covered the summit plateau and spilled over the sides. Table Mountain takes on a new dimension when its cloth is on the table! This can be viewed from a distance, particularly from a boat in Table Bay.

Blaauwbergstrand, a beach twenty miles to the south afforded the whole panorama of Cape Town's mountain surroundings. This I found out when I visited Cape Town sixty years later in 2016. I had not visited Blaauwbergstrand when I lived in Cape Town. On our visit my wife and I were nervous about walking along the beach. There were no other whites present. We were watched intently by loitering blacks.

Marta said nervously, "I don't want to stay on this beach the locals look threatening."

We visited a number of other iconic sites I missed out on in the Cape Town area in 1958. These included the Cape Peninsula containing the Cape of Good Hope and the penguin colony near Simon's Town. Marta and I waited for the funicular railway carriage to take us to the end of the Cape Peninsula. I got talking to a white, tallish lady in her forties guiding a pair of visitors.

I complained, "Could they not have spared the Peninsula from urbanisation. When I was last in Cape Town sixty years ago the lovely surroundings were far less developed."

She replied indignantly, "People have to live somewhere!"

The party from the Devonshire Hill Hotel reached the top of our climb through the *kloof*. It was apparent that the summit plateau was not as level as the name Table Mountain suggested. We were greeted by a broken landscape of valleys and hills. These were generously covered with a mosaic of plantations of exotic conifers and indigenous shrubs and small trees. Dispersed among these were open *vlei* areas (marsh). Near to the centre was the Woodstock Reservoir whose dam afforded us a crossing point. Overlooking this change of scene we settled down to eat our sandwiches accompanied by the fruits of the Cape which the hotel had provided. I tried to get our climbing party to line up for a photo.

"While you are assembling that would make a better informal picture."

One of the girls, Gillian, was rather voluptuous, although she was significantly taller and older than me, with dark hair

The author and climbing party from Devonshire Hill Hotel on top of Table Mountain. Photo taken by Ivan, Cape Town, 1958.

and an appealing face. I must say I rather fancied her. Try as I might I could not catch her eye. She was well spoken clearly her home language was English. Jill undoubtedly had a job in the city and like all the residents of the hotel, except me, lodged in the main building. I assumed I was not good enough for her, too young, and without any income. Well, you can't win them all!

I joined the University Mountain Club so that added to my knowledge of Table Mountain and other peaks around. Unfortunately there was a preponderance of males in the club. That did not detract from the great excursions and wonderful exercise scrambling up Table Mountain by different routes. Table Mountain must be one of the few mountains in the world that has everything close by. It had a splendid climate and incredible vistas. These included oceans, beaches, the busying of ships around the port and of course the proximity of an iconic city. The mountain was in the backyard of this city. The splendid University was the icing on the cake.

One thing I liked about the mountaineering club was that it seemed dominated by the older years. It was more in concert with my early twenties. What girls it did contain were the more athletic kind, well-equipped, not in sexual endowments, but for mountain walking with hobnailed boots. No high-heeled types here. Having said that I don't know what some of them got up to in the balmy Cape evenings!

Wider explorations around Cape Town

Next to the University was the zoo which seemed rather appropriate as I suspected that some of the students went a bit wild at times. A visit to this menagerie was with Jackie, a tall slim lady in her thirties from the Devonshire Hill Hotel. She accompanied the hotel party up Table Mountain earlier. Jackie seemed fond of duffle coats and long trousers.

The animals of this site reminded me that I had neglected to read zoology at Cape Town. This seemed a pity as I had studied the subject at Acton Tech, West London. Something had to give in my full timetable. Anyway by so doing I managed to avoid making a dog's dinner of my dissections.

The centre of attraction at the Zoo was the lion's den rather than Jackie who was a rather plain Jane, but good company. The magnificent animal in this enclosure looked rather forlorn. He did not have company which seemed to highlight the problem among some of the people I met in Cape Town.

Jackie said, "It seems ironic that when the first white settlers arrived in the Cape Town area, some four hundred years ago, lions were roaming about here. Now no lion in the

Catching our breath after a climb. Mountaineering with
Cape Town University on Table Mountain, 1958.

A rare lady in UCT's mountaineering club.

wild exists in South Africa within one thousand miles of Cape Town Zoo."

Lions occurred in the Kruger National Park and surroundings but that was near the north east extremity of South Africa. Lions have been reintroduced in recent years to game reserves further south. The Zoo was not only enlivened by Leo but bird cages resplendent with the exotic plumage of species from the Bushveld of southern Africa. The surroundings were enhanced with a background of gardens and pinewoods.

A large area on the lower slopes of Devil's Peak had been preserved for posterity. This was done through an endowment of the will of Cecil Rhodes. He seemed to be behind many of the initiatives in southern Africa. Through Rhodes the University found a grand site. Monuments, a world-famous botanical garden and an iconic house known as Groote Schuur (the Great Barn) benefited from the protection of the site. The title Great Barn seemed to be the utmost understatement. The building dates from the early settlement of the Cape. Later modifications turned it into a superb, old, Dutch colonial style mansion. This residence was none other than the home of Rhodes, the Prime Minister of the Cape. Later Prime Ministers of the Union of South Africa and the Republic which succeeded it occupied the house. All these wonders were close to my digs at the Devonshire Hill Hotel!

There are plenty of examples in Britain where beautiful escarpments, incredible viewpoints, have been saved by farsighted benefactors from urban blight. So it was that Rhode's estate preserved the lower slopes of Devil's Peak from encroaching urban development. However, I noticed on my visit to Cape Town in 2016 that the lovely pine covered slopes of this area had been hacked about in places. This I understood was due to black squatters. They presumably were recent arrivals swelling the population of Cape Town from the upheavals in Zimbabwe, formerly Southern Rhodesia, and elsewhere.

Prime Minister's residence, Groote Schuur, Cape Town, 1958.

A friend I made in Cape Town was Joe, a man in his early forties, a recent arrival from Britain. He walked about in a business suit even at weekends. Apparently he was a bit of a ladies' man. He heightened my interest in the opposite sex by embroidering stories of his sexual encounters with young white women in the "Tavern of the Seas."

One particular meeting he found memorable because it whetted the appetite of the lady. I don't mean he took her out to dinner. No doubt that was part of it.

Joe said, "She enjoyed sex so much that she pestered me repeatedly for more."

I said, "I feel sorry for the lady although I have never met her."

I believed that if a man takes advantage of a lady in this way she wants to make a permanent relationship of it. Some would say Joe was a cad although I cannot talk as I had leanings in that direction later.

I found Joe's company pleasant. One of a number of Cape Town highlights we visited was Groote Schuur and its splendid gardens backed by groves of magnificent Mediterranean pines.

Rhodes Memorial was another highpoint of my exploration of the lower slopes of Devil's Peak with Joe. It celebrated the life of Cecil John Rhodes and embodied a horse with rider entitled "Energy." We ascended the steps to this temple like structure embellished. This was rather too much of an energetic exercise as far as Joe was concerned.

He said, "Must we go on these walks? A taxi would be better."

This modest ascent was rewarded with views across Rondebosch with the Hottentots Holland Mountains in the background.

Not long before I revisited Cape Town again in spring 2016 the media in Britain carried articles about student unrest at Cape Town University. There were calls for the removal of Rhodes Memorial because they saw Rhodes as an imperialist and oppressor of the blacks. The memorial was removed. This was in spite of the huge contribution Rhodes made to South Africa and university education in particular. In autumn 2016 the British media carried accounts of a black student from South Africa who won a Rhodes' Scholarship to Oxford. When he got there he demanded the removal of Rhodes' statue at the university. Fellow Oxford students agitated for the removal of this ungrateful scholar's scholarship. If the attitude of the South African students was followed to its extreme conclusion much of the writing on world history would be obliterated. Even universities that were too open- minded would disappear.

An even more ambitious climb, at least as far as Joe was concerned, was up Signal Hill. I am being unfair here because I was half the age of Joe. This hill was barely one thousand feet high, a lovely companion to an even higher hill known as Lions Head. But modest height can afford splendid views, all the more rewarding if you had toiled to the top under your own steam.

Joe was a bit of a gadget buff, rather like my mate Dave in the Sabi Valley, Rhodesia. He was into cine cameras when I could barely afford a still camera. Joe often sunned himself on the lawn just in front of the Devonshire Hill Hotel showing off his cine camera to other guests. More significantly he had a tape recorder. Such items are taken for granted by the majority of the population in Britain today. They are of course in a much more sophisticated form than sixty years ago. Joe was some sort of journalist. That explains why he had a tape recorder. I took advantage of that technological marvel. I tried to get the tape recorder working.

Joe scolded me, "No not like that. Thread the tape through here."

I said shyly, "I don't like gadgets. They are so finicky."

Recording my experiences in Cape Town, I mailed the reel to my family in London.

When I returned to my London home some years later I was rather put down by my sister Margaret over my recording on the tape.

She teased, "You sounded like Ralph Wightman on the tape."

He was a radio presenter in Britain before I left for Africa. Televisions had barely been acquired by the general public at that time. Ralph Wightman had a distinct West Country accent. He was more a country yokel some would say. He discussed all matters rural. Whether I felt I must speak in an affected way on such a recording device I will never know.

While in Cape Town I purchased a Frejus bicycle with the word embellished on its frame. Being a sports bike it was light weight and accompanied by an incredible number of gears, far in advance of any bicycle I had in Britain. This was necessary for the rugged terrain of the district. But I certainly did not use it for racing, just generally getting around.

This was long before crash helmets were worn by cyclists or even those that drove Vesper scooters that seemed to be everywhere in Cape Town. Looking back I wondered about the wisdom of such transport. Motorists in southern Africa, whether white or black, were well known for a blasé attitude to motoring.

I thought Frejus was an appropriate name on my bicycle because it was the name of a resort on the Mediterranean coast near the French/Italian border. I was constantly drawing parallels between the two areas in my mind, the Med and the Cape.

I must have looked somewhat out of place in Cape Town on my Frejus bicycle, sporting a blazer with Acton Technical College, London, badge emblazoned on it. Additionally I had long trousers. Shorts did not seem appropriate when attending university, even in a sub tropical country. University papers were stuffed under my pullover and a book lodged in my pocket. My friend Joe admonished me for looking so slovenly.

Why do I look so serious, but studious with
my university papers? Cape Town, 1958.

"You should tidy yourself up. Cape Town is a dapper place."

"You forget I am a student not a well paid business man like you."

Students the world over can look rather eccentric, compared with the general population. That is the luxury of being a student, nonconformist and somewhat rebellious.

Alan was another mate who accompanied me on my rambles through Cape Town, a rather heavyweight young man in his early twenties. He worked at the Groote Schuur hospital a mile or two from the Devonshire Hill Hotel. The hospital had an outdoor swimming pool set in magnificent surroundings, below the brooding pine clad heights of Devil's Peak. Here we swam from time to time. Alan was not impressed with my swimming.

The author standing by Groote Schuur Hospital staff pool. The world's first heart transplant was performed in this hospital shortly afterwards in UCT's medical school. Cape Town 1958.

"You over exert yourself. In that way you are too tired to progress further. Take it more gently."

The hospital was associated with the medical school of the University. But that was the least of its distinctions. Here Dr Barnard and his team performed the world's first heart transplant on a human, a short time after I left Africa. He no doubt practised on animals first. The transplant patient only survived a week or so, due to the complications of rejection. Here the recipient's body reacts to something that is foreign to it. That operation was a miracle no matter how short the success was. It was a magnificent start and went from strength to strength by the perseverance of Barnard and his team. Other surgeons throughout the world took up the challenge. Today such a miracle of medical science is routine now that the problems of rejection have been overcome. Practice makes perfect!

The Rag

There was a much more immediate miracle of science and technology that was celebrated in Cape Town at the time of my residence. This was feted in the University rag. Students at universities and colleges, the world over, regard the rag as the climax of the academic year. It is an excuse to show off. It advertised that the academic institution was not just a stuffy old collection of buildings in which students and staff engaged in esoteric exercises. They were not out of touch with the outside world. Their work had relevance to the here and now.

Invariably a rag is topical, celebrating a current event. So many students from Cape Town University had been busying themselves for many weeks in their spare time. They were drawing, painting, cutting, gluing, all manner of materials to make floats, models, dioramas, mounted on motorised vehicles and horse-drawn carriages. These were draped with alluring young lady students strutting their stuff.

The great day arrived and a procession of floats made its way from the campus towards the city. Down Cape Town's premier thoroughfare of Adderley Street it went. Here crowds from far and wide had gathered, not only along the pavements but on the balconies and windows high above the street. They comprised a melee of widely contrasting groups, not only whites but blacks as well. There were English speakers and Afrikaner whites, but also Cape coloureds, Malays, Africans with fascinating archaic faces, remnants of the Hottentots and Bushmen.

One middle aged, full of figure, white lady next to me said, "I don't believe it!"

"What do you mean?"

She explained, "I don't believe there is a whatnot hundreds of miles up there. If there was it would fall down. It is a con!"

The theme of the Rag was the incredible feat of the Russians to put a Sputnik in space, the first artificial satellite to orbit the Earth. It encircled it every few hours, one hundred miles or more above its surface. It advertised its presence with an indescribable radio signal.

University of Cape Town rag, on theme of Russian Sputnik, moving through central Cape Town, 1958.

When I was working in Rhodesia, Dave my mess mate said, "I actually saw the Sputnik last night as a faint moving point of light!"

Such a feat had implications that were not fully realised by everyone at the time. It sent shivers down the spines of Americans and launched the space race. No doubt the scientists and technologists of the University of Cape Town were even more excited than the general public. The new Department of Astrophysics had barely left the stocks at Cape Town University. It was no doubt fully aware of the uses of such technology. The Russians had "pulled a white rabbit out of the hat."

I attended the University rugby match at Newlands, a famous rugby ground not far from the college campus at Rondebosch. This was another occasion when I renewed my acquaintances with the ladies of the University displaying their charms. I was not over enthusiastic about rugby. I had never played the game and I always associated it with public schools, expensive fee paying schools in Britain. In South Africa it was different, as it was a game that the nation as a whole embraced, at least the white population. I thought a visit to the Newlands rugby ground would be illuminating, an insight into South African society. I was not disappointed. The American atmosphere of the occasion impressed me. There was a troop of drum majorettes, recruited from the female students, who strutted their stuff. The cheerleaders encouraged the whole proceedings along. They had appealingly tight uniforms complete with short skirts.

One beefy student next to me on the stand said, "You should take more interest in the game than taking pictures of the drum majorettes!"

CHAPTER 8

WINDING DOWN AT CAPE TOWN

University dates and study concerns

My dates in Cape Town were not confined to the more mature business ladies from the Devonshire Hill Hotel but also girls from my university classes. Denise and I made a day of it on the beach at Seaforth, near Simon's Town on the Cape Peninsula. Denise was a slim, petite, young lady, rather modest.

Authors date, a Cape Town University student,
Seaforth, Cape Town, 1958.

She said when I pressed her about her academic work, "I am embarrassed to talk about my studies."

To any considerate beau such a discussion would have been off the agenda. Ladies want to be comforted, admired, especially on first dates.

Seeing her discomfort at my questioning I said, "I am uncertain about my progress at the University. A chat on this topic would relieve the weight on my mind."

In theory I should not have had excessive concerns as I had studied one of my three Cape Town subjects, botany, at Advanced level in Britain. True at evening classes, while fully employed. I noticed there seemed to be a fairly close overlap in the content of the botany lectures and practicals in the two countries.

British students applying for entry to Cape Town University were required to have passed the examinations necessary to enter a British university. Two A-levels, Advanced Levels, were required in addition to the equivalent of the South African matric. So in some ways I was repeating at Cape Town a standard of education I had experienced in Britain, at least in one subject. It did not seem like it. This was because of the different emphasis and shorter time frame.

Qualifications were only part of my reason for going to Cape Town. University life, its ambience and that of an iconic city and an incomparable environment were immeasurable. Letters after one's name and a passport to a professional career seemed secondary. So it has proved because I have never forgotten that year at Cape Town.

No doubt Denise, my date on the beach at Seaforth, would like to think I was focusing on her. Young females soon forget what their dates have told them about what they have done, no matter how adventurous. They remember how their dates have made them feel good about themselves.

My second date from Cape Town University, who I also took to Seaforth beach, was even shyer than Denise, although

I cannot talk. Sheila was another petite girl. My five feet five inches height could hardly entitle me to otherwise.

She said, "I don't want you to take any more pictures of me."

Sheila kept turning her face away from the camera. I only had a photo of the back of her head and her attractive form below her neck.

The Navy at Cape Town

Close to Seaforth beach, where I snatched a few hours of solace from my brief encounters with female students, was Simon's Town. This port on the Cape Peninsula had long been associated with the British Royal Navy, as a servicing station. It was in a strategic position. Here the South Atlantic approaches the Indian Ocean. It was a kind of Gibraltar of the southern hemisphere.

The Suez Canal seemed threatened during the Second World War. Later in the fifties Egyptian ambitions overwhelmed it. Simon's Town's value was enhanced. It was on the route from Europe to the Far East.

The British Navy was not the only fleet that showed the flag at this extreme southerly tip of the African continent. This continent blocked oceangoing vessels from moving west to east and back for many parallels of latitude. It had the second largest landmass of the continents.

The United States Fleet commanded the adjacent waters of the South Atlantic. It put into Table Bay from time to time. These were courtesy visits honouring the host country. It brought welcomed income to the local businesses from sailors on shore leave. Pepping up the love life of the young ladies of Cape Town was an added bonus.

There was another advantage that the American Fleet brought in and that was a show of force. Here was a flexing of the muscles, a strutting of the stuff. It was a message to those lookouts, spies, who frequented such important ports as Cape

Town. The United States was not a country to mess with. Indirectly of course such a message implied that "Uncle Sam" was prepared to protect his friends. This was especially when such a friend as South Africa was rich in minerals. These included those of great strategic importance of which uranium was but one.

I toured the flight deck of the great aircraft carrier *Essex*, moored in Duncan Dock, bristling with aircraft with folded wings and surrounded by protecting firepower. There was a myriad of accompanying warships. This was one of the highlights of my stay at the Cape.

The American South Atlantic fleet put into
Cape Town on a courtesy visit, 1958.

Protests at the University

A particular friend I had at Cape Town University was Charlie Chan. He was a postgraduate student in his early twenties. As his name suggested Charlie was of Chinese origin, although born in South Africa. He had one of the highest honours in judo, a black belt no less, a very useful means of defence in any situation. We visited various points of interest in Cape Town and around.

Cape Town University did not admit non white students. This policy was more related to that of the South African Government rather than the University. The Nationalist, Afrikaner dominated Government, dictated the strict separation of the races. It put pressure on the South African universities to uphold this policy of separation.

The exclusion of non-Europeans from these universities did not include Chinese. The non-whites of South Africa were provided with a university of their own, Fort Hare.

There were students at Cape Town University and apparently staff who felt strongly about the exclusion of their black brothers. Feelings ran so high that some students staged protests. These were no doubt closely watched by the South African Police. No prizes for guessing who was among those protesters! Some would argue that I should have been more careful. I needed to keep a low profile. This was especially when I was known to the South African Police for entering the country without getting my passport stamped! I protested on the steps of UCT and in procession in the heart of Cape Town. That was not the only occasion when I dabbled in politics in South Africa. Another year had to pass for that!

End of year exams

The Christmas holidays were fast approaching at the end of the academic year. Shortly before were the University's examinations. I wended my way up the flight of steps that ascended the lower slope of Devil's Peak, towards the Jameson Hall. The glorious sunshine announced the start of summer. This belied the fact that I and a host of other students were about to take our place in the examination hall. I turned round, at the top of the steps, before entering the Jameson Hall. I took a last look at the wonderful scene before me.

I glanced over the suburbs of Cape Town, to the Hottentots Holland Mountains on the horizon. They were stark and shimmering in the heat.

I made up my mind before that stage that I could not continue at the University. My money was running out. I had obtained a small loan from the University. I took a long time to pay this back. This was not prudent in view of the interest.

Just as I was about to enter the Jameson Hall I was wished good luck by one of the demonstrators from the practical botany class. She was a more mature lady than Kay McGill from the geography practical. I never seemed to get near to Kay in spite of encouragement when I first registered. Perhaps she saw I was not promising enough either academically and/or in other attributes.

Although I believed I had prepared well for the examinations, I did not have high hopes. Everything seemed to disappear from my head as soon as I sat down. My mind was as blank as the writing paper in front of me. I hardly noticed the liberal sprinkling of young female students in their summer dresses. They were casting nervous glances at each other, but in particular at the young men around them. No doubt trying to make a lasting impression on someone they fancied before it was too late. Who was to know whether there would be an opportunity to return to that magnificent place?

In the last few weeks of my year at Cape Town I had scanned the situations vacant in the local newspaper. I spotted an eye-catching spread for a technician in the laboratories of African Explosives and Chemical Industries. This company manufactured dynamite for the mining sector, part of the huge Anglo-American Corporation. This organisation incorporated De Beers of diamond mining fame. Their advertisement was "Diamonds are for-ever." I sent off the completed application form to their branch in Somerset West, just outside of Cape Town, where there was an explosives plant.

Bar tendering reveals all

The long summer vacation was upon us. Incongruously for one used to snow in Britain at that time, Christmas was celebrated in the heat of summer. It was an uncertain period at the end of the academic year. A time before the exam results had been announced. Indeed it was before I received notification of my application to African Explosives. During this holiday I became a bartender at a hotel. Though poorly paid, this was my first income since leaving the employ of the Rhodesian Federal Government, almost one year earlier.

There were other student workers from UCT at the Van Riebeeck Hotel, named after the founder of Cape Town. The hotel was a rather unimpressive three-storey modern building on the front of Gordon's Bay. This was a small resort with a harbour, some twenty miles outside of Cape Town. Behind the hotel rose the Hottentots Holland Mountains which I had often seen from the campus of the University. They changed their appearance with the seasons, even with snow covering its higher parts in winter.

The proprietor of the hotel was a heavily built character in his fifties. He was an overpowering man, not only in stature but also character. He did not suffer fools gladly. Mr Stern was recognisably a Jew. He undoubtedly ran the hotel efficiently. He did not make it a relaxed atmosphere for the staff and me in particular. After university study and examinations I had hoped my few weeks at the delightful resort of Gordon's Bay would be a bit laid-back.

There was a very definite rule regarding the serving of customers according to Mr Stern. If they asked for a brandy, even if the brand was specified by the customer, they would always be served Olde Meister. This was no doubt because some concession existed between the hotel and the supplier. With some difficulty, as regards my conscience, I would pour the recommended drink out of sight of the customer. Sometimes I would get my brands mixed up, much to the consternation of the ever watchful Mr Stern!

One day a tall, lean, sun tanned man in his thirties sat down at the bar opposite me. In a Rhodesian accent, with a slight smile on his face, he ordered a drink. It turned out that Jim was a policeman on holiday from the Rhodesian police.

I said enthusiastically, "I left the Sabi Valley Experiment Station in Southern Rhodesia a year ago."

Immediately his interest was aroused. Noting his reaction I thought I would press Jim on a subject that had puzzled me.

I said quietly, "Our chief suddenly left us unceremoniously without apparently giving notice to anyone?"

Jim gave me the startling news, "Dr Conway was wanted by the Rhodesian Police!"

Naturally my interest took off at this revelation. I did not believe I would get a definitive answer to my obvious follow up question without encouragement.

In consequence I poured Jim another drink saying, "This is on me."

At this the ever watchful Mr Stern drew nearer. His ear seemed to grow bigger as he strained to catch every word of our conversation. Noting this I lowered my voice to almost a whisper.

I uttered the burning question, "What was Dr Conway wanted for by the police?"

Jim's rejoinder was more sensational than his opening sentence, "He was wanted for misconduct with Boy Scouts in the Salisbury area two years ago!"

This reminded me that Conway disappeared right in the middle of my exile in the Sabi Valley.

Jim volunteered the information, "Dr James Conway fled to America. He was a citizen of that country. He presumably got wind we were on his tail."

This revelation helped to sort out in my mind the eccentricity that our chief apparently displayed at Sabi. It raised other questions in my head such as whether others at the research station knew of his misdemeanours. To me Conway fell into the macho category of men judging by his assertive behaviour which fortunately had no direct impact on me. That it is possible to lead an organisation without abrasive assertiveness was illustrated by Dr Conway's replacement the pleasant Tom Jones.

The other macho character at the Sabi Station was the engineer Jo Butcher. He physically assaulted me because his wife gave me a lift. This I Interpreted was related to unfaithfulness on the part of Jo Butcher. The nature of this unfaithfulness was unknown to me. Macho men are often controlling men. They are known not necessarily to confine their sexual attentions to women.

In my chance meeting with Jim of the Rhodesian Police I was tempted to make a statement. This was about the physical assault on me by Butcher. Considerable time had elapsed after the event. The need to preserve goodwill with a former employer was an important consideration. I would require a reference should I be considered for another job. This made me think twice about reporting Butcher to the police. So I never did.

I had not come across cases of homosexuality in Southern Africa until I learnt about Conway from Jim. Apparently homosexuality is un-African behaviour. To my knowledge it was un-African during the time I was in Africa. So presumably Conway did not try it on with the blacks. I also understood that homosexuality was not accepted at the time of my residence in Africa in most countries of the world. In the twenty first century it is a different matter. Sexuality has been turned upside down. Apparently Cape Town is now the gay capital of Africa. When I was there in 1958 I never saw or heard a word on the subject except what I heard from Jim in the Van Riebeeck bar.

It seemed sad that that Dr Conway experienced a downfall. Here was a man who had contributed greatly to agricultural research in central Africa and also apparently in Alaska. Both areas owed much to pioneers in both the geographical and scientific sense. I had no direct contact with Dr Conway. Viewing him from a distance he seemed overbearing.

The day dawned when the examination results of UCT were published, so on one of my breaks, from my alcoholic duties, I visited that splendid pile. I bumped into one of my lecturers, who seemed to take some interest in me.

She stated without even referring to any records, "You have passed the theory papers of your subjects, but the results of the practicals are close to borderline. I will look forward to seeing you in the new academic year."

I did not wish to disillusion her on that point, "Thank you for your inspirational lectures. Have a Happy New Year!"

Back at the Van Riebeeck I felt somewhat deflated. I pondered on my uncertain future, so much so that I did not join whole heartedly in the partying.

The girls said to me, "Take a more active part in Christmas and New Year celebrations."

They had the added exuberance of examination successes and the financial means to return to the university.

I spent some time in my hotel room assembling my large collection of photographs in an album. These I had taken over the previous three and a half years. They included my journey from Britain to Rhodesia, my explorations of Southern Africa, and life in Cape Town. Even this record, detailed in white ink under each photograph, would have an adventure of its own, which at the time I had no inkling.

There was one particular girl with whom I struck up a friendship at the hotel. Mavis MacKenzie was a pleasant brunette of average proportions and attractiveness. Invariably she would be accompanied by a tall, slim, dark haired girl, a fellow student who also worked at the hotel in the University long vacation. On occasions I managed to get Mavis alone. I walked her down to Gordon's Bay harbour to watch the sun go down over the South Atlantic.

Mavis had just received the good news that she had graduated, passed her Bachelor of Arts degree from UCT in sociology. Mavis wanted to serve as a social worker among the blacks of the Cape.

Gordon's Bay, near Cape Town. Colleagues from
Van Riebeeck Hotel at end of UCT course, 1958.

I made a pass at Mavis which she seemed to enjoy.

Because I cut it short she said, "Was that too biological for
you?"

I thought that comment was a bit below the belt. After all I
had studied zoology, but not at Cape Town. The rabbit was
the closest animal to a human I got to in my studies!

The next morning, close to the bar where I worked, Mavis
appeared with a frown on her face. She was in the company of
a tall hefty student. I had earlier given him a wide berth for no
particular reason other than his size and somewhat threatening
demeanour. He broke ranks with Mavis and coming up to the
bar admonished me in a thick Afrikaans accent.

"You took advantage of a young woman when she was
most vulnerable, exciting her sexual instincts and then broke
off." Jan continued, "Mavis disappeared into her room
un-consolable!"

This lecture played on my conscience. I thought this
outburst illustrated the strict religious upbringing of those
Afrikaners who followed the Dutch Reformed Church.

The incident with Mavis reminded me of the warning the Reverent Heck gave me in my early teens in London in my confirmation classes.

He said, "You should not excite young ladies where they are most sensitive!"

My mother had further advice for me on the same subject. This was when I returned to London from Africa and I cultivated British girlfriends.

She said teasingly, "If you don't like the goods don't muck them about."

This I believe was a cockney expression when she was a shop assistant in her youth.

The prospect of an explosive career

A few days before Christmas I received a letter with a Somerset West postmark, the industrial town some five miles from the Gordon's Bay hotel. I recalled that my application for a job with the Anglo American Corporation, the great South African mining and explosives manufacturing giant, had a major branch in that town.

With some trepidation I tore the envelope open. The letter had an impressive logo and announced that it came from the office of the chief chemist, African Explosives and Chemical Industries, A E C I. It said, "We request your presence at an interview for a laboratory technician post at 3pm on December 23rd, 1958." Was I about to be saved from my situation overseen by Mr Stern at the Van Riebeeck Hotel?

On reaching the company site I was greeted by massive chimneys, chemical steel containers, and glistening pipes of the great industrial plant of African Explosives. I was directed into a spacious room, and asked to sit in front of a long polished table. Opposite me were assembled a dozen white, smartly dressed men of various ages. The chairman introduced himself and the adjacent gentlemen who appeared to have papers in front of them. These apparently included my CV in the form of an application form.

The Chairman said, "Could you please outline your technical experience."

I described my laboratory work in London, Rhodesia and at Cape Town University amounting to over six years. This was followed by questions. It all seemed to impress many of those present.

The question which stood out in my mind was not technical at all. I was asked about my mountaineering experience which I had briefly referred to on the application form. I summarised my climbing of the highest mountains in Britain, Rhodesia and of course Cape Town's iconic eminence, Table Mountain. I emphasised I had been a member of the University of Cape Town's mountaineering club. It seemed to me that the questioner of my climbing experience was leading me on to other areas for consideration. The interviewer was emphasising the idea of challenge as applicable to the workplace as much as to the mountains. I got more than an impression that this interview was not just geared up to determining the suitability of a candidate for a job behind a laboratory bench. It appeared there was the potential for higher things. Here initiative was tested and the ability to work alone as well as in a team!

The interview turned out to be the most thorough I had ever encountered. But that was not the end of it. Following there was a battery of tests directed at intelligence, manual dexterity, and speed of reaction. I was certain I had failed, particularly as I felt threatened by a man in a white coat. He watched me attempting the intelligence tests. At the same time he held a flickering finger over the button of a stop watch. I nearly throttled this character and stuffed his clock down his throat followed by the exam paper I was trying to complete. I held my nerve. Reviewing this situation some time later, I felt this was a means of determining one's reaction under pressure. This gruelling intellectual assessment had all the hallmarks of American methods of staff selection. I wondered how the company could regard themselves as so special that they could adopt such techniques. Again hindsight was to answer that question.

After Christmas but before the New Year, 1959, I found a letter in my pigeonhole at the Van Riebeeck Hotel with AECI embossed on it. I was so overcome with anticipation that it took awhile for the full import of the communication to sink in. I was offered the post of scientific and technical officer in the laboratories of African Explosives and Chemical Industries. This was a subsidiary of the Anglo-American Corporation of South Africa. The company director I saw from the heading of the letter was Sir Ernest Oppenheimer. His name was well known in economic and financial circles of the City of London. Western shareholders held such an individual and company in high esteem. But of course such "insider" knowledge was unknown to me at the innocent age of just twenty three.

These revelations seemed more than enough to digest that I hardly noticed the two following paragraphs. I assumed the post would be at Somerset West, a stone's throw from my beloved Cape Town. In that I was mistaken! I was to proceed, as soon as possible, to the company's largest industrial plant. This was at Modderfontein on the north-east outskirts of Johannesburg.

I had barely familiarised myself with Joburg only a year earlier. This was during a lightning tour of South Africa's largest city. It was the largest conurbation, the Witwatersrand, at that time in the whole of Africa. This city had more Europeans than any other in the not so Dark Continent. My visit was on my hitchhike from Rhodesia's Sabi Valley to Cape Town University, a distance of some two thousand miles.

The third paragraph of my offer of employment suggested I contact Somerset West to arrange a mutually convenient time to join the company. It went on to state a rail warrant for the thousand mile journey from Cape Town to Johannesburg would follow shortly. I would soon be posted across the breadth of the subcontinent. I would become an employee of a huge, powerful organisation. The company had a finger in every pie related to mining and chemical engineering. This was the case not only in South Africa but well beyond its borders. It had interests in the Federation of Rhodesia and Nyasaland. Together with South Africa this encompassed an area equal to one third of the United States.

A cold call on Muriel

A date was fixed in early January, 1959, for my departure from the Van Riebeeck hotel, and the start of my new career in Johannesburg. I decided in the interim period to pay a visit, on a day off, to a friend of my father's sister Milly. Aunty Milly had worked with Muriel in London until she had migrated with her husband to South Africa.

Wellington, where Muriel lived, was a small town of some four thousand Europeans and only a little more than that number of coloureds. It was thirty miles north east of Cape Town. I did not make an appointment. Telephoning from a box seemed too laborious. It was four decades before mobile phones arrived. I wanted to explore the area as I understood it was mountainous, on the lower slopes of which were vineyards. This was a distinct lure as I was rather fond of wine and I had plenty to celebrate! I figured that if Muriel and husband were not at home it did not matter as I could wander about the town. Perhaps I could get drunk on the cheap plonk! Thirty miles might seem a long way to go on the off chance. I was used to serendipity and my lift got me there in no time.

It was a typical South African bungalow which stood before me. The garden was profuse with floral colour. What intrigued me was the name by the side of the door "Alberta Lodge." Alberta I knew was a province in Canada at the foot of the Rocky Mountains.

A pleasant, buxom looking lady, in her fifties, came to the front door. Her husband looked bemused as he peered from an inside door.

A typical couple and their bungalow, Wellington,
near Cape Town, Jan 1959.

Before I could say a word she took one look at me and
almost spat out, "Not today thank you!"

I assumed my rucksack and student looking appearance put
her off. I sported a dark blazer with the imposing gold braided
badge of Acton Technical College on it. This no doubt led her
to believe I was filling the long vacation with a little hawking.
Cold calling was a favourite source of income for students in
the holidays.

Somehow I blurted out, before she could slam the door in
my face, "I am a relative of Milly Hardy."

It was as if this utterance was an "open sesame" to any
difficult situation. This stopped Muriel in her tracks. She
momentarily checked the door before it closed for ever on our
relationship! But the full import of my exclamation did not

sink in instantaneously. I assumed from this she had not clapped eyes on Aunty Milly for some years.

I followed up by reminding Muriel, "You were an old colleague of Milly and I understand a close friend. I am Peter Hardy, Milly's nephew."

This supplementary introduction did the trick. I was soon joined by her husband, a tall, slim man of similar age to Muriel.

I sat down with Ben in the sumptuously furnished lounge while Muriel made tea. I gave a brief summary of my adventures in South Africa, including my stay in Cape Town.

When I stated, "I have just got myself a post with the Anglo-American Corporation," Ben's interest seemed to take off.

It was obvious the company was held in high esteem in South Africa.

It was not long before the question was asked what salary I expected. Under normal circumstances I would have been cagey about this. Different people have a different take on such personal subjects. You give too low a figure and people ridicule you. On giving a sum that most people could not aspire to then you encourage jealousy. How could an insignificant creature like me deserve such recompense?

I had no knowledge of the going rate of pay for South African Europeans (whites). I was therefore interested in Ben's and Muriel's comments. So I told them what my pay would be. Ben and Muriel were astounded.

Ben said, "You should grasp their offer of appointment with both hands as it is a very generous salary!"

Ben apparently had some executive post in Cape Town which involved a thirty mile commute on the railway. He appeared to be in a good position to judge the kind of salary that a young man such as I should expect. Armed by the comments of Ben and Muriel about my new found wealth my confidence leapt!

I gently enquired, "Why is your delightful bungalow called 'Alberta Lodge'"?

Ben said enthusiastically, "Muriel and I spent a holiday in the Canadian Rocky Mountains. The log cabin where we stayed impressed us with its ambience and magnificent surroundings. We named our bungalow in memory of that holiday."

Four decades later my wife and I shared a similar experience among the peaks, lakes and forests of Alberta in a log cabin.

It was not the "Blue Train" that I took from Cape Town to Johannesburg. That luxury snake of carriages sped along the thousand miles of track. Only the richest and most discerning passengers had that privilege. My more modest train was perfectly adequate for my purpose. There was a dining car and a berth for the night. The journey took more than a day!

CHAPTER 9

DYNAMITE IN JOHANNESBURG

Alchemy at Modderfontein

After one academic year, 1958, at Cape Town University, I started work at African Explosives and Chemical Industries, part of the Anglo American Corporation. AECI was a very extensive industrial plant situated at Modderfontein on the north-east edge of the urban sprawl of Johannesburg. The factory manufactured explosives, in particular dynamite, for the large mining enterprises of what was then the Union of South Africa. Chemicals associated with explosive manufacture at Modderfontein included the fertiliser ammonium nitrate and nitro glycerine. The plant was a mass of chimneys, pipes and tall iron towers. Aromas of ammonia and brown fumes of nitrogen dioxide were continually wafted into the air. Nobel, a Swedish scientist, invented dynamite in the 19th century, after whom the Nobel Prize was named.

Beyond the nucleus of the industrial plant were mounds of turf with entrances to tunnels. Here were stored the explosives, manufactured on-site, ready for dispatch. These mounds were substantially far apart and linked with a network of roads. Such spaciousness was to prevent a chain reaction should one of the dumps explode.

Dispersed through this "parkland" were dams (reservoirs), some of which were a hundred metres long. Water required in great quantities on such a large factory site. This was not only for cooling plant excessively heated by chemical reactions but in the reactions themselves.

The dam area was landscaped, planted up with trees, particularly on the verges of the larger reservoirs. I remember walking round one or two of these large lakes with a friend I made while working at AECI. Harold was a well built chap in his mid twenties from Yorkshire, England. His wife and child were waiting to join him in South Africa after he got established.

Harold (left) and author by reservoir. Dynamite factory, Modderfontein, Johannesburg, 1959.

Harold was an engineer. I particularly remember Harold because he taught me to knot a tie properly. A distinct improvement on a "granny knot" that usually materialised from my efforts to make myself presentable! I always made a dog's dinner of my knots in the 5th Ealing Scouts, west London!

Harold would say, "Peter, you need to smarten yourself up by making a proper knot to your tie. You will never get a girl at that rate!"

I got the impression that Harold had more experience of partying than me. Appropriate dress was second nature to him.

I worked in the extensive laboratories as an "experimental officer." This post was concerned with quality control of chemicals used in the manufacture of explosives and fertilisers. Even the paper wrappings in which they were packaged were tested. Like the laboratories of the Pyrene Company, London, my first employment after leaving school, AECI used American methods of research and development. In consequence both companies seemed ahead of their times.

There were different sections in the Johannesburg laboratory with a small team of technicians assigned to each group. They carried out tests on different components of explosive and fertiliser manufacture. I was put in sole charge of a small laboratory housed in a room next to the large main laboratory where most of the technicians worked. I assumed I was given the responsibility of my own laboratory in Joburg because I had similar responsibility at the Sabi agricultural research station in Rhodesia. This was in the two year absence of my line manager, the soil physicist. He had disappeared into the desert surrounding Salt Lake City in the U S A. He was researching the effects of salt contamination on irrigated soils on behalf of the Rhodesian Government. Whether his head was turned by living among the Mormons, I will never know. This is a religious sect believing in having more than one wife simultaneously. No doubt his wife he brought from Rhodesia would put a brake on that!

Life beyond the alchemist's den

I was accommodated at the African Explosives complex in a rather splendid, tastefully built, one-storey building with the grand title of "Drakensberg Hall." It was perched in a prominent position surrounded by large palm trees. This must have housed up to one hundred staff, mostly technicians, but

I also believed some professionals: industrial chemists, physicists, and engineers. My room and the accommodation in general was a distinct improvement on anything I had experienced in Africa previously.

I made some friends at Drakensberg Hall. One particular friend, Bill, was a tall, heavily built, fair haired chap in his early thirties.

He said one day, "I can see you're interested in photography but you should up-date your camera. I have a German camera that is surplus to my requirements. I can sell it to you for a knock down price."

Drakensberg Hall. Author's Hall of Residence, Modderfontein
Dynamite Factory, Johannesburg, South Africa, 1959.

The author, Johannesburg.

So I acquired an up-grade of my photographic capabilities.

Not long after my camera purchase I bought a light meter. This as the name suggested was used to tweak the settings on my camera to get pictures of maximum clarity. I now felt I was in the same league as professional photographers. Enthused with confidence at sporting photographic gadgets suspended with belts outside of my bush jacket, I was ready to take pictures of the wildest of animals.

Bill, my photographic friend, offered to drive me to the River Vaal one weekend. This is South Africa's greatest river, just fifty miles south of Joburg. Checking the light with my new meter on the edge of the river bank the meter slipped and disappeared into the Vaal! It must still be there to this day.

Bill seeing this said, "Sorry Peter, I have not got a second hand one to sell you this time."

Meals were obtained from a large self-service canteen near to Drakensberg Hall which catered for every taste and palate. Canteen customers, not just the residents of the industrial site, but other employees of the company who lived in Jo'burg beyond the company, were exclusively white.

Adjacent to the canteen was a large hall with a stage where amateur theatricals were presented, particularly at Christmas, in which employees took part. The hall also showed films, not necessarily the latest from Britain and America. I recall the music from films including *Seven Hills of Rome* in which Mario Lanza sung.

Occasionally I saw a film at a public cinema in the centre of Joburg which was often quite a new release. One I remember was called *The Bridge on the River Kwai* with Alec Guinness. It was about the use of British prisoners of war by the Japanese. This involved building a railway bridge out of bamboo high over a jungle river durng the Second World War. Some of the POWs destroyed the bridge just as the first train was passing over it. It was based on a true story.

This film had a rather catchy marching tune. I hummed and sung this on the occasion of missing the last evening bus to Modderfontein after the film. I therefore had to walk in the dark the six miles from Joburg's centre through the north-eastern suburbs, largely composed of white residents' houses. More alarmingly I passed the black location of Alexandria, a notorious black residential district. This was beyond the last white suburb. I told Bill about this.

He said earnestly, "It is unheard of for whites to make such a journey alone, on foot and in the dark. Joburg is noted for its brutal murders, mainly black-on-black."

A formula for this discontent was a mixture of tribal members: Zulu, Xhosa, Shona, Ndebele, to name but a few.

Bantu from all over South Africa, Rhodesia, Nyasaland and Mozambique and even beyond were expected to be buddies. These were mostly males away from their rural kraals, perhaps one thousand miles or more distant. They had been attracted by the promise of good money compared with what they got from cultivating their village plots. These earnings were well below that earned by the whites on the mines and its ancillary industries.

One weekend Harold, the Yorkshire engineer, and I went to watch a mine dance in Joburg. Male black workers from the gold mines stamped their feet in deafening unison. Different tribes put their interpretation on it.

Harold shuddered, "They are big chaps. I would not like to cross swords with them!"

Lovers on the Reef

The song "Three Coins in a Fountain" I heard in a film in the Joburg explosives factory. It referred to the wish for a valentine, a lover. On this note I had two girlfriends while on the Witwatersrand, the gold bearing ridge or Reef on which Johannesburg stands. I seemed to acquire these young ladies rather mysteriously and the circumstances of this are a bit hazy. As I remember I got an invitation from the parents of each of these teenagers. I was twenty three at the time. This was to have tea but really to meet their daughters in the parental home. There was no doubt the parents hoped their daughters and I would make an item. Apparently the fathers were employed at the dynamite factory, presumably in senior posts judging by their homes. Somehow they got to know me at some function on the company's premises and presumably believed I was wholesome enough to date their daughters. As they were English-speaking as opposed to Afrikaners they probably thought I would be more acceptable for their daughters.

June I met first, a rather plain seventeen-year-old. Lack of makeup made her look plainer. Lack of colour in her clothes enhanced the unattractiveness. I had great difficulty in communicating with her in the lounge of the parental home, no doubt within earshot of her parents.

I said, "June, what do you like doing best."

I was not sure what I meant by this. I was just trying to make conversation.

Jean retorted, "Knitting!"

I did not believe this. She was too young to have this as a hobby. This encounter fizzled out before it barely began.

My second date was entirely a different matter. Maria was born in Holland of Dutch parents, who migrated to South Africa a few years later. Maria spoke perfect English, and she had other admirable qualities. She had a stunning figure, medium height, blonde, voluptuous, extremely well endowed and with a friendly disposition! The problem was she was only fifteen! On the face of it eight years difference between partners is not particularly remarkable. I am eleven years older than my wife. Maria I assumed was below the age of consent.

I was not familiar with the law of South Africa with regard to sexual matters. I knew it was illegal for whites to have sex with blacks and that the police made regular patrols enforcing this law. They snooped on people. At night they shone torches on courting couples in cars. It was rather like King Canute sitting on the beach and demanding the tide stop! The moon may affect lunatics but there is no doubt it controlled the ocean's tidal movement!

What I did know was that African girls became pregnant practically as soon as they could bear children, which was substantially below the age of fifteen. Europeans (whites) in South Africa were a different matter. I was surprised that Maria's Dutch parents encouraged a relationship between us when their daughter was of such a tender age. The Netherlands was noted, particularly in recent years, for its broad minded attitude towards sexual matters. Afrikaners, South Africans of early Dutch origins, from a strict Protestant background, the Dutch Reformed Church, had the opposite view.

There were a number of considerations here that might not be apparent to a bystander viewing this affair from a distance. I was not particularly forward in sexual matters. I was more interested in the great outdoors and getting myself an education that would equip me for an interesting profession. In the meantime I hoped to gain geographical and scientific knowledge through my serendipitous discoveries of places and jobs. This has been a feature of my life up to that time and indeed ever since. The journey became more absorbing than the arrival at a destination.

The other consideration, likely to be overlooked by a pontificating, hypothetical bystander, was that Maria's parents were probably concerned about her because she was so "ripe." Because of her innocence she was likely to attract the sexual attentions of men. Her parents wanted to marry her off before she fell foul of a man who had no interest in her as a person but only in her body!

Maria confided one day, "My parents like you. They want us to be friends."

"That's a very nice thing of your parents to say. I'm sure we are going to get on fine," I replied.

Maria's parents presumably saw in me a level headed fellow who would look after their daughter. Parents, I imagined, were not concerned with their daughter's lack of experience with men. They wanted to get them married off as soon as possible to a suitable suitor, not one who regularly sniffs around different women. After all civilised humans are not like the animals of the African bush mating with the first female they encounter who is sexually mature and receptive. The Afrikaner nation, as I understood it, was even more concerned with choosing a suitable mate. This was undoubtedly because of their religious beliefs as members of the Dutch Reformed Church.

In a cynical mood I would say there was a more pressing reason why Maria's parents took a particular interest in me. Indeed this was likely to be the case with my earlier girlfriend June. This was because I worked for the prestigious African Explosives and Chemical Industries Company. It was well known that they paid their white employees well. In my case more than well for they seemed to have been impressed with my track record. Whether the parents of my Joburg girlfriends had inside knowledge of my salary I was unclear.

The population of Johannesburg was growing fast not only attracting blacks from far and wide but also whites because of the job opportunities it offered. These people needed to be housed and the whites were particularly discerning in the accommodation they required. In consequence there were high-rise blocks of apartments mushrooming up around the central business district, many of them of a desirable nature. The leafy white suburbs were growing too, filled with attractive bungalows with colourful gardens.

I got the impression that mortgages were readily available to purchase these desirable residences especially if you worked for AECI. These considerations must have weighed heavily on the minds of the parents of my two girlfriends.

Voluptuous Maria knew that I fancied her. Any young red-blooded male could not possibly have helped it. I had great difficulty in controlling myself in the parental home when her parents were in the next room. Maria could see this.

She said one day, "Why don't you buy a car Peter. You could take me on lovely drives into the countryside."

This was undoubtedly an invitation for us to get away from her parents, even for a few hours.

I said to Maria while trying to stifle my excitement, "The thought of enjoying your company in private conjures up all sorts of fantasies!"

With this I kissed her full on the lips my tongue searching for an opening to her mouth. Maria flung her arms around me pressing her body in mine.

Practically every other white adult had a car in South Africa at that time long before this was the case in Britain. This was not just because South Africa had a higher standard of living than many parts of Europe. The country had a wonderful climate conducive to driving about. These were great incentives for whites to migrate to the Union. Feeding the demand for cars was the country did not have a dense enough network of public transport. Where it existed the buses were mainly used by blacks.

I never did get myself a car while in Joburg. This was largely because I did not want to commit my finances to such an outlay. I had another use for my savings which was taking shape in my mind. Anyway if I had got a car I might have got Maria into trouble and been accused of baby snatching!

Fun in the park

I continued to divide my spare time between visiting Maria and going on excursions with Harold. This was before Harold's wife and child joined him from Britain. One occasion was when Harold and I paired up with two South African, white, young women in their mid twenties.

Cable car view of zoo and built up area, Johannesburg. 1959.

Agricultural show, Johannesburg.
Fearsome looking cattle in foreground.

Caledonian Society dancing (Scottish), Johannesburg. 1959.

Harold wrapped up for Johannesburg's winter.

Johannesburg is cold in winter, as my overcoat makes clear,
because the land is one mile above sea level.

Using technology to milk cows, Transvaal. Some Africans
performed a variety of responsible jobs in a European led economy.

"Harold! How about us taking the girls boating? I know of
a terrific lake in a Joburg park," I enthused.

On phoning the girls Margaret said, "I know that park.
There are braaivleis (barbecue) stands there. I could buy some
meat and rolls for us."

We enjoyed a day out in one of Joburg's splendid parks.
The park in the northern suburbs was of sufficient size and
greenery to make a welcome change from the industrial
location of our work. Getting away from the little Manhattan
appearance of central Joburg was also a welcome break.

Charlotte & Margaret. Tea in the park, Johannesburg, 1959.

Harold, Margaret and Charlotte, Johannesburg, 1959.

Author with Johannesburg girlfriends. War memorial behind.

The park had a particularly large lake rather like the Serpentine in Hyde Park in central London and like it was particularly good for boating. We hired two rowing boats. Harold and I each had a popsy in our boats. I drew the short straw with a rather plain lady. Charlotte was a brunette, tall and slim, but as she wore slacks I never got to know whether she was leggy in any attractive sense. Her friend Margaret was in an entirely different category, medium height, black locks, and voluptuous. The latter quality was enhanced by her shapely legs. Harold was clearly pleased with his afternoon's female acquisition.

Our boats were propelled through the water, in my case by my own efforts at the oars. Charlotte reclined opposite me indifferent to my struggle to point the boat in any meaningful direction. Her disinterest I suspected was due to her detecting I did not fancy her. Harold had a short stint at the oars. I noticed his head came surprisingly forward towards Margaret's top at the appropriate point in the oars cycle!

I heard Malcolm say to Margaret, "Please change position Margaret and have a practice at the oars."

He leaned attentively towards her seemingly to instruct her in the art of dipping her oars. On all these occasions, opportunities, I tried to steer my boat close to Harold and Margaret. When successful I discovered Harold was getting an eyeful of her full breasts by peering down her loose top! Lucky chap!

Meanwhile Charlotte looked even more displeased, no doubt because of my lack of interest in her. After all we were in the same boat together. Additionally her friend was getting more than her fair share of attention, not only from Harold but also from me. I frequently snatched jealous glances towards the accompanying boat. This was more particularly towards the antics going on in it. No doubt Charlotte was infuriated. I had probably been written off by Charlotte as a bore. Not the Afrikaans word with similar pronunciation, namely a farmer, but a tedious person, even a kind of peeping Tom!

I said to Charlotte, "This boating experience is getting too much for me. The physical demands of rowing are overpowering."

Charlotte ignored the remark. There was no offer to take over from me. Also there was the complete unfairness of the situation. Harold had collared a most attractive girl while I was not so lucky. Adding salt to the wound he was a married man and I was single! Harold already had a lady stashed away in Britain together with their child. By all accounts they would be joining him soon in sunny South Africa!

Then I noticed the source of my jealousy disappear under some weeping willows fringing the shore. Harold and Margaret remained there for several minutes while I rested on my oars in the middle of the lake. Charlotte looked more and more disgruntled. Harold and Margaret then emerged from their hideaway. Harold rowed in a much more determined way than before.

I heard him murmur, "That was exhilarating getting close to you."

He seemed elated by his experience in the bushes while Margaret looked equally happy.

Drawing alongside us Harold reminded me and Charlotte, "We are going to have a South African barbecue in the park after tying up our boats."

Harold and Margaret on Joburg park lake.

We headed for the boat parking lot.

Most recreational areas in southern Africa had barbecue facilities, bricks built up to form a support for a grill under which a fire could be made. Thereby *Boerwors* (Boer sausages), and strips of pork or even game (wild animal meat from the veld) could be grilled. The girls had generously provided us with such delicacies. These were newly acquired from the butcher in their parade of shops in Joburg's flatland. Here were high rise blocks of apartments for singletons. They had the advantage of shopping more readily in the great department stores and more specialised shops that central Joburg had to offer. People in the suburbs had their local shopping centres.

In no time our steaks were sizzling merrily.

Margaret said, "I am putting Harold and Peter in charge of the bangers."

Barbecue in Joburg park with Harold, Margaret and Charlotte.

It required more than a little reminding by the girls that we had to turn them over regularly. The bangers I mean. Harold and I had our minds elsewhere whenever Margaret bent down to adjust the steaks! Sausages like sex had and have different names.

The wife arrives

Not long after that memorable day in the park Harold's wife arrived with child in tow.

Annette, a pleasant, well built lady, said, "I am a little nervous of the new life I am about to start. It looks quite different to England."

The "single" life that Harold had enjoyed for some time, which apparently gave him a new lease of life, abruptly came to an end! It occurred to me that this was a salutary warning to me not to get married too early. A young man's ambitions can be severely curtailed by the responsibilities of married life.

My fifth form master, Mr Scannell, the last teacher I had before leaving my school for the world of work, reminded the class of this truism.

He said earnestly, "When you get married you are likely to be submerged in raising a family. The chances of improving your educational qualifications are likely to be severely reduced." Banging his hand on the desk he emphasised, "You had better do as much learning and gain as many O-level passes as you can. Do this before you leave school! You are unlikely to do this afterwards!"

Somehow I treated this wisdom rather seriously and passed several non science subjects at O-level while at school. The school did not teach science and had no 6th form for A-level study, no means of preparation for university entrance.

Against all the odds I passed science O-levels and A-levels and gained a B.Sc. Honours degree of London University. This was while working as a technician before getting married. I then continued to prove my fifth form master wrong in his advice. I went on to gain two other London University degrees and two teaching certificates. This was while I was married with two daughters and employed full time. My London fifth form teacher was a successful poet indeed he became famous for his poetry and novels. He was a champion boxer of the northern universities. Vernon Scannell had to interrupt his university studies to fight in North Africa in the Second World War. He inspired me to love poetry.

To celebrate the arrival of Harold's wife and child in South Africa and colleagues families in a similar situation, a party was arranged for them. I was invited along together with about eight other couples. The problem was who was going to be my partner at the party? As stated before I had two girlfriends in Joburg. I realised I could not take Maria because, although stunning, she was at fifteen too young to promenade in front of the party guests. The average age of the guests was thirty and besides it was likely to be a very alcoholic affair. South Africans and those aspiring to be South Africans were noted for knocking back the hard stuff at any opportunity.

I had no choice but to consider my least favoured girlfriend, one I had neglected to take out for some time.

I said to June on the phone, "Would you accompany me to a party welcoming the wives of colleagues to South Africa?"

To my surprise she agreed. It occurred to me later she might have thought this was a precursor to a proposal. This was because I made it clear that it was a party for mostly married couples. June was seventeen. I wondered whether I was leading her astray in such a boozy environment. She contented herself with a soft drink. I, a man of advanced age, in comparison, namely twenty three, decided not to have anything more alcoholic than a Castle Lager.

It was difficult to conceal from June that I did not fancy her. Girls are quick to detect such things. She retaliated by moving down the table so she was next to one of the wives of the guests. It was made clear we were not an item. She was probably only at the party to indulge her curiosity as to the company I kept and to catch the eye of any other possible single man. This was no doubt at the behest of her parents. They were clearly anxious to get her married off to someone else with prospects. Networking on such occasions creates all sorts of marriage possibilities. No doubt June was sadly disappointed that everyone there was spoken for.

I had a grasshopper attitude to life, serendipity, sampling everything that might broaden my knowledge of the world in a scientific and geographical sense. I was not over concerned with sensual, romantic, or material things. This was an impediment to "settling down". Parents with daughters, when they got to know me, would soon realise I would not make a good catch.

CHAPTER 10

A GRILLING FROM THE CHIEF CHEMIST

"Sexpot" inducts me

Before performing tests in my own laboratory I had a very rapid verbal induction. My instructor was Isabel, a technician a few years older than me. She was a plain Jane, slim and tall.

Isabel said to me when I was titrating, "You need to copulate slowly, one drop at a time!"

Titrating was a method of determining the chemical concentration of liquids. Hopefully copulating needs no explanation. It seems that sexual intercourse has so many different names depending on the company you keep. They varied from the more polite term of Isabel to the crude! It appeared Isabel, "Sexpot", fancied me, a maverick who had breezed in from afar.

She said, "You are different to the majority of young South African technicians in the main laboratory. Did you have a girlfriend when you were in Cape Town?"

Isabel's attempts to gain my sexual interest seemed to get in the way of her instruction, the science I mean! She seemed more concerned with making a sexual impression than revealing the mysteries of the chemistry of dynamite! Isabel wanted to have a big bang with me, without the aid of explosives!

What concerned me about all this was that nothing was written down, the methods of chemical analysis I mean! Laboratory tests of a routine nature are often spelt out in government printouts, British Standards in the UK. This is so the new technician performed the tests in exactly the same way as a previous occupant of the post. With the new technician working on his own this is even more important. In a team situation he can turn to a colleague to remind him on a point. Otherwise errors can creep into the determination, biases peculiar to that particular operator.

"Sexpot" would say when she had described a test without demonstrating it, "Now I have told you how to do it." She would then sidle up to me. When I moved away, disliking her physical contact, she looked annoyed and said, "I will describe the next test."

But again no demonstration was given. If I did not take an interest in her she would only give me the bare minimum of scientific instruction. It was sexual blackmail. Those were the days when sexual harassment was an unknown subject. I would have been laughed out of court if I suggested I was being sexually harassed by a woman! Today, in the 21st century, sexual harassment is headline news in Britain, usually harassment of a woman by a man!

In my experience, a laboratory technician's work varied considerably from one company to another. The scientific apparatus might be similar for carrying out those assays. The glassware in most chemical labs was similar: measuring cylinders, pipettes, burettes, conical flasks etc. The determinations varied according to the products that the company was concerned with. Up to that time, January, 1959, I had analysed electroplating compounds, fire extinguisher chemicals, road construction materials, soil and toxic elements affecting crops. Now I was expected to analyse explosive materials.

A laboratory technician who moves from one employer to another has a core of scientific knowledge. This has to be adapted considerably to the changing products he deals with. I believe that many employees, including laboratory technicians, stay a long time with one particular employer. This I believe is because they do not want the stress of learning new routines particularly as they advance in age. The attitude "You cannot teach an old dog new tricks" is powerful. By holding that view they are not stimulated by new challenges. They become comfortable, set in their ways, complacent and smug. Such people feel they know everything there is to know about their "little neck of the woods." Really they are big fish in a very small pond!

"Sexpot" was complacent and protective about the knowledge she had. She was not going to share it with me without my cooperation.

"She said the boys in the main lab have all got wives or girlfriends."

The results of analysis, which I submitted like the results from the main analytical laboratory, were ultimately sent to the office of the factory manager. This office monitored the quality of the manufacturing process. This would be adjusted to compensate for any variations from the norm indicated by the analytical results. Such criteria as the strength of the chemicals and their paper wrappings were involved. This data was filed away. I found this out some time later. Sexpot certainly did not tell me. I would have had to shag the living daylights out of her to get that information.

I could see why my interview in the company's plant near Cape Town was so thorough. Workers had to be conscientious, hard-working and skilful. A company that pays for an engineer to come six thousand miles from Britain to South Africa needed to be sure what they were getting. This was the case with Harold, my engineer friend.

I found out later because of the early responsibility of my job in Joburg, I had just turned twenty three, I was well paid. This was in comparison with most other lab technicians at Modderfontein.

"Sexpot" kept reminding me, "Mable, your predecessor, left to have a baby. I could have had one but my boyfriend left."

I briefly met Mable sometime afterwards when she visited the laboratories to socialise with former colleagues. She was a rather plump woman, in her late twenties. To what extent her fullness of figure was due to pregnancy, absence of exercise, diet or more precisely lack of it, or genetics, I was not sure! It would have been more appropriate if Mable had inducted me rather than sex mad Isabel. If this had been the case I presumably would have got a more "hands-on" induction, used in the professional sense, rather than a sexual innuendo. I would have had time to ask questions and even make notes. Perhaps time to enquire whether there were any printed descriptions of the tests.

The ability to memorise technical detail or indeed any detail varies from one individual to another. In my view this is not necessarily related to intelligence, for one can understand quite difficult concepts without having a head for memorising detail. The recognition of this cognitive quality by educationalists, in recent years, was made aware to me when I became a teacher. This happened some years later after obtaining my first degree.

The sixteen to eighteen age group of secondary schools and colleges of further education took national exams, GCSE and A-level, in Britain. They were often given data in the exam papers which they had to analyse and comment upon. Data in many cases needed to be memorised in former years, without prompting in the exam paper, and then commented upon. In later years "sympathy" on the part of the examiners resulted in much less emphasis being placed on the ability to memorise facts.

It was rather like an actor on a theatre stage, or indeed in the making of a film, not bothering to learn his or her lines. He or she knew the prompter was hidden away in some recess, now a-days perhaps some devious electronic means. He was always on hand as a safety net to remind the actor of some part of his or her lines, or indeed all his lines in some extreme cases! There had been a revolution in the need for memorisation, at least in some sectors of education. At that distant time in my lonely laboratory in the Joburg dynamite factory such a consideration would no doubt have been laughable to the powers that be!

Impending doom

At a very early stage in my scientific career at Modderfontein, Johannesburg, I was summoned to the chief chemist's office. This came as a bit of a shock. I was escorted by "Sexpot" who had inducted me in a hasty way. Scientific instruction of me was not her priority. She had made sexually loaded words while doing it, the induction I mean.

What was embarrassing was we had to thread our way through the main laboratory where the majority of the technicians were located. They must have sensed I was being frogmarched into the hallowed presence of the chief chemist. A number of eyes focused on me, accompanied by bemused creases in their faces. This was given a sinister twist by the sea of white laboratory coats. It almost suggested I was about to be confined to some mental institution!

I expect my colleagues were pleased to have a diversion from their bench work by witnessing the proverbial sacrificial lamb about to be slaughtered! Their interest was heightened possible by grievances they harboured. I, an upstart, a young Britisher, a *roinek* (redneck) had walked into a job that many technicians in the main lab would have coveted. It was likely that I was better paid than many of them due to me running my own lab.

The Chief Chemist told me later, "Do not reveal your salary to anyone."

To add salt to the wound of those that might envy me, this upstart had just left a prestigious South African university.

Here he had only completed a year and earlier entered South Africa illegally from some bush job in the wilds of Rhodesia.

True I could not be sure my fellow technicians were in command of all these facts. These considerations flashed through my mind as I walked towards the head chemist's office. But those were not the only thoughts that troubled me as I followed "Sexpot" round the benches. They were littered with all manner of compounds of explosives being tested for consistency in their manufacture.

I had been appointed as a result of an intensive selection process one thousand miles away. This was near to Cape Town in the company's explosives plant at Somerset West. However, the post was in Johannesburg. In other words I had been appointed over the heads of the senior personnel staff in Joburg including of course the Chief Chemist, Mr Schwarzkopf. This must have rankled particularly with the latter gentleman. A possible indicator of this was the chief chemist or his deputy did not greet me on my arrival. Perhaps I was being presumptuous in my expectation.

This scenario reminded me of the situation at the Sabi agricultural research station, Southern Rhodesia. I was appointed lab technician there as a result of an interview in Salisbury the capital, some three hundred miles from Sabi, by the Station's soil physicist. This was without input from other staff at the Experiment Station. The Rhodesian Government wanted my line manager, the soil physicist, to update his knowledge of irrigation through work in the USA. This was among the Mormons, the strict religious group which believed in polygamy. In my wildest dreams I wondered what it would be like to be married simultaneously to plain June, better to have called her Jane, and voluptuous Maria! The repercussions of favouring one wife at the expense of the other could not be imagined.

The lab techs and chemists' eyes were riveted on me. They were no doubt straining their ears for an indication of Mr Schwarzkopf's mood should his door open. His room was raised above the level of the laboratories he commanded. This gave an uninterrupted view of his empire.

We arrived at the hallowed door of Mr Schwarzkopf B.Sc. Wits., a chemistry graduate of Witwatersrand University, Johannesburg.

As if to emphasise my predicament "Sexpot" said to me, "Hardly any lab. tech. enters the Chief Chemist's room. Only the most senior chemists and the factory manager had that privilege."

The door opened at the hesitant knock of "Sexpot", with me in close attendance.

Schwarzkopf was a tall, slim man of about fifty years of age. He beckoned "Sexpot" and me to take a seat while he sat down behind a massive desk. His "in" and "out" trays contained a huge pile of papers. This was long before the existence of personal computers, internet and emails. It was rumoured that massive, wizard like machines existed, with magical properties of manipulation, which could number crunch at the speed of light. Apparently they were hidden in the bowels of a few research institutions in America and Europe. These could hardly be practical for the office, let alone home use, like personal computers today.

I noticed on Mr Schwarzkopf's desk a number of graphs which I assumed he had recently been studying. A glance revealed a much more massive man, but of similar height to the chief chemist, in an almost cloistered corner of the room. Presumably he did not want to be seen.

Schwarzkopf turned to "Sexpot" and said, "Miss Ayers please summarise the instructions you have given Mr Hardy on the laboratory tests." He continued but in a sarcastic tone of voice, "This was in the hope Mr Hardy would subsequently be able to carry out the work."

"Sexpot" gave a rambling catalogue of technicalities.

She said, "I have repeatedly explained the tests to Mr Hardy. He said he could not hear everything I said. He kept moving around me so what he called his 'good ear' was pointing in the right direction."

"Sexpot" leaves me

Schwarzkopf thanked "Sexpot" for her resume and said she could leave, this of course implied that I was to stay! For once I wished I could hide under "Sexpot's" skirt and follow her out the door. Thereby I could avoid the massacre that I was sure was to follow. I would have done anything to satisfy "Sexpot." If only she could have saved me from that situation! "Blackhead," for that was the translation of his name, fixed his raging eyes on me. He gave me a copy of the graph he had in front of him.

I should explain, that Schwarzkopf's name did not mean he was black. He was white, like all the scientific staff in the laboratories. There may have been up to forty laboratory staff including professional chemists. As the Chief Chemist's name suggested their ancestors may not have all come from Britain.

The Chief Chemist said, "I hope you will notice from the graph that your analysis of glycerine is erroneous."

Glycerine combines with nitric acid to form nitro glycerine, which is very explosive, even from the slightest knock. To drop it on the floor gives it sufficient impact to blow the laboratory and its contents to smithereens.

Schwarzkopf continued even more expressively than before, so that I thought he would explode even without the help of nitro glycerine.

He pointed out, "When your results from duplicate samples were plotted they were way off the graphical line. This showed the margin of tolerance in experimental error. These are small biases resulting from the use of different analysts, lab. technicians."

The Chief Chemist explained, "The analytical results of the laboratory staff were monitored. The same sample that they analysed some time before would be returned to them in a different guise. They were given a different sample number. The analyst would believe it was a new sample. It was rare for a technician to get results that were miles off of the target!"

I was tempted to interject in my defence saying that "Sexpot" had rushed through the instructions. She had diverted my attention with sexual innuendoes. Sexpot was not the most recent occupant, if she ever was, of my little Joburg laboratory. The previous one had disappeared before I arrived on the Witwatersrand to have a baby. She was apparently unlikely to come back. So I did not get my instruction from the "horse's mouth" or a sympathetic ear at my elbow to answer any questions.

"Sexpot's" oral instruction was likely to have been a watered-down version of the pregnant lady I replaced. It was a bit like the line of pre-First World War soldiers who passed a message from the back to the front. This was, "We are going to advance" which became, "We are going to a dance."

However, I felt I could not launch into all these excuses, at least not at that stage. This would have raised the hackles of the management. They would have interpreted this as an attack on the senior officers of the high security dynamite factory. Proper training of staff is fundamental to any business especially one as sensitive as AECI. The Chief Chemist would probably have had a rap over the knuckles for lax supervision of his laboratory staff. I was wise enough to perceive all these repercussions in spite of my tender age at the time. So I took Schwarzkopf's criticism on the chin.

The crunch came when the Chief Chemist asked me, "What is the explanation for your erroneous results."

At this question the shadowy figure in the corner of the room, who I had noticed earlier, leaned forward. He appeared to strain his ears. No doubt desperate to ascertain how, if at all, I could defend myself! Later I discovered this large character was the deputy head chemist. It was obvious he was being used as a witness. Nowadays mobile phones and even more subtle electronic methods are witness to what people say.

This is not only used by criminals but the general public on people they do not like. People are increasingly coerced into conforming. It questions whether our so called democracy is in fact just that.

I had to say something to this witheringly pointed question. So I replied in a hesitant, contrite way that I felt was needed for the seriousness of the occasion. I imagined Schwarzkopf, appropriately for his name, was soon to put a black cap on his head and dismiss me to death row!

"Thank you for being patient with me and giving me an opportunity to speak," I said.

This seemed an unexpected response. Somehow the number of creases in "Blackhead's" face and that of his deputy decreased slightly. They were partially replaced by a quizzical, almost bemused look.

I paused, and on the spur of the moment decided to water-down all the criticisms of the training programme. Presenting them in as low a key as possible seemed the right thing to do. My opening sentence in my defence followed.

"In my experience as a laboratory technician I always had a file of notes on the tests that I performed," I explained.

It flashed through my mind by making such a statement that I sounded like a seasoned scientist, experienced beyond my twenty three years. This could well have been the case compared with colleagues of comparable age in that Johannesburg lab. They might not have ventured, professionally speaking, beyond the confines of the Witwatersrand.

I added, "My notes were provided by the establishments in which I worked."

This was far from correct, for my lab in Rhodesia's Sabi Valley was the only employer up to that time that provided this prudent aide memoir.

I had come across a laboratory methods manual issued to University of Cape Town students while I was studying at UCT. However, that was not quite the same as having notes in a job.

My two inquisitors, one actual and one potential, winced at the points I made. I had not made a direct attack, but the implications were clear.

Following up I said, "I was given a comprehensive set of chemical and physical scientific test notes at the Sabi Experiment Station in Rhodesia. This was because the soil scientist in Rhodesia had left me to run the laboratory on my own in his absence in America. There was no other staff member at the experiment station to offer me any advice should I have got into difficulties. In fact there were no difficulties because the laboratory manual he had compiled was explicit in every detail. My absent line manager was professional." I could see I had well and truly scored a goal!

Icing was added to the cake of my argument.

I expounded, "I am well aware of the nature of the factory in which I work. There is the need for high security and sensitivity in the training of personnel dealing with explosive materials."

Schwarzkopf's face and that of his deputy turning red at this muffled shot across the bows. The implication of my oblique criticism could not have been lost on my bosses. They no doubt realised if these got through to their superiors they might be in hot water for not arranging adequate instruction for me.

Saboteur paranoia

On returning to my Johannesburg lab after the weekend I found a new inductor. She was clutching a manual on the laboratory testing of components of explosives. Being a mature lady she did not divert my attention to the task in hand by uttering sexual innuendoes. After a day or so she took leave of me. I attacked the tests with an earnestness that knew no bounds!

In spite of me turning over a new leaf I noticed Schwarzkopf shadowing me on a number of occasions. He was apparently doing chemical and physical tests on a bench within eyeshot of the open door and window of my laboratory. I had never seen the Chief Chemist doing laboratory bench work before, no doubt he had left his laboratory practical tasks years before. He was now concentrating on shuffling papers in the sanctity of his office with his door securely closed. It was obvious Mr Schwarzkopf was doubtful about me! I was not sure whether he wanted to intimidate me. Certain types of people, like dogs, conscious of any suggestion of timidity in others, want to undermine them. Schwarzkopf had reason enough to do this for no doubt he could have been on the carpet for not arranging adequate training and supervision for me.

There was an additional explanation for the chief chemist's suspicious mind. South Africa was very sensitive to saboteurs. These were those who wanted to throw a spanner in the works of South Africa's economic progress, which was increasing by leaps and bounds. These agent provocateurs were numbered among those people who disagreed with the government's racial policies. The explosives plant at Modderfontein was an indispensible factory in the mining sector, a bulwark of southern Africa's economy. The government was mindful not only of protecting the nation against external aggressors but also of internal security!

British settlers were well-known for having a more liberal view on the racial question than the Afrikaners. They had been great empire builders. Understanding and cooperation with the native people was the cornerstone of maintaining their empire for as long as possible. The days of gunboat diplomacy were beginning to look old-fashioned to them! But this was apparently not the view of the majority of the Afrikaners. It was certainly not the view of the Nationalist government, overwhelmingly dominated by Afrikaners. Industry, African Explosives being a prime example, was more liberal in its views. This was because it was run largely by English speaking South Africans, management and workers. But these like the English speaking universities of South Africa had to pay lip service to South African government policy regarding race relations.

The Communists were not an insignificant force in South Africa, and Jews were numbered among them! They favoured the rise of the blacks who had for too long had a raw deal. But many whites and no doubt industrialists were fearful of the consequences of embracing such politics. The advancement of southern Africa had depended on the supremacy of the whites. They were the initiators, the creators of modern South Africa!

America and Europe were casting envious eyes on the apparent monopoly of South Africa not only in gold and diamonds but the new wonder elements. These had strange properties called radioactivity. The "uraniums" of the earth promised to give possessors of such magic supremacy of the world!

As time went on I noticed Schwarzkopf seemed to be tailing me less frequently. He was not setting up a chemical analytical ruse close by. I interpreted this as a cover to carry out surveillance on my competence. There came a time when the Chief Chemist was rarely seen in the laboratories. He seemed to return to confining himself to his room. No doubt mining through the mountain of papers I noticed in his "in" tray when we had our electric meeting some weeks previously.

Then as if a bolt from hell our paths met on one of my jaunts through the main laboratory. We were watched by the white coated chemists and physicists of whatever rank and knowledge. It was as if the great white wizard, for I always regarded chemistry as the modern product of alchemy, had engineered a brush with me. But to my surprise it was not "Come to my office at once" but a friendly greeting. This was immediately followed by a more welcome utterance. It was delivered in a low voice, for my close encounters with the boss always seemed to elicit interest among the lab staff.

Then, with an almost unheard of smile on his face he said, "Your laboratory results are consistently spot on. They do not waver from the line graph." I could scarcely believe my ears.

Immediately my stride gained extra impetus, and my posture gained extra height.

In writing this it reminded me of what a senior colleague said to me. I was teaching in the largest comprehensive (all ability school) in London years later. He was a fellow collector of British Empire stamps.

Jim said, "I felt ten feet tall, proud to be British, when our army yomped across the Falklands. It was a world away from Britain. They defeated the Argentinians. How dared they invade a British colony?"

Explosive encounter in the lab

In between enjoying my weekend's venturing into the back of beyond I continued my work of testing dynamite and its components at Modderfontein. I also continued to tiptoe around the parental home of my fifteen-year-old girlfriend.

I had apparently now a clean bill of health as far as the Chief Chemist was concerned, or so I thought! I grasped any excuse I could to break the confinement of my personal laboratory. I sauntered across the main laboratory in spite of the fact that my white clad colleagues still gazed at me with bemused looks. They were no doubt conscious that I was not Schwarzkopf's favourite technician.

On one occasion I was making my daily jaunt, ostensibly to visit the wash room. I weaved among the benches decorated with all manner of analytical chemical glassware. There were bubbling retorts, distillation equipment, and fractionating columns separating a chemical compound into its constituents.

I entered a laboratory hived off from the rest, similar to mine, but with a through passage.

The middle of this room had not been reached when the young technician working there accosted me with the words, "Hi catch!"

I was conscious of a long brown object whizz past my ear. It hit the floor with a dull thud and ricocheted in the direction of the main lab. that I had just left. It caused my colleagues there to have a much bigger distraction than my encounters with "Sexpot" and the Chief Chemist. I swung round to observe the trajectory of this object. It began to take on the appearance of a comet from deep space, a harbinger of doom, judging from the faces of my colleagues. Their bemusement had been overtaken by horror. It at first appeared to be a large candle wrapped in thick, glossy, brown paper. In another instant it resolved itself into what was clearly a stick of dynamite. An appearance I was familiar with when it was stationary.

But that was not the only calamity that "The slings and arrows of outrageous fortune," to paraphrase Shakespeare, had to hurl at me. The offending object had come to rest at the feet of none other than the Chief Chemist. He had apparently been walking only a few paces behind me. I had no time to recover from this invasion of my personal space when a voice boomed out.

It uttered, "van der Merwe, come to my office immediately!"

I never saw Pete van der Merwe again! I have no recollection of knowing him earlier in any meaningful way, positive or negative. I interpreted his behaviour as being related to the unfortunate human behaviour of giving someone a kick when they are thought to be down!

Throwing a stick of dynamite at someone might seem like the end of the world for that person and any infrastructure around him. Without a detonator and the means of firing it, perhaps an electrical impulse, the explosive will not explode. So analysing the components of explosives was not as dangerous as it seemed. That is provided they were not in an assembled state!

Nyasaland and Northern Rhodesia Trek, Jul/Aug, 1959

Introduction

This is an account of a three week hitchhiking trip I made alone from Johannesburg, South Africa, to Nyasaland and Northern Rhodesia, present day Malawi and Zambia respectively. It was during a three week statutory holiday I had accrued from working as a laboratory technician in African Explosives and Chemical Industries. This was part of the Anglo American Corporation, where I was employed for one year in Johannesburg.

I decided to explore Nyasaland and Northern Rhodesia because they had not formed part of my adventures in Southern Rhodesia, where I worked earlier, or my explorations of South Africa. These explorations included a two thousand mile hitchhike from my technician post at the Sabi Valley Agricultural Research Station, S.Rhodesia, now Zimbabwe, to Cape Town University, South Africa. It was a circuitous route taking in the main components of South Africa and described in this book, Book 2 of my Trilogy.

While in Johannesburg I wanted to visit a corner of southern Africa that reflected the continent before it had been changed much by the white man. So I decided to investigate an area wilder than South Africa. I was going to hitchhike back to the Federation of Rhodesia and Nyasaland. Visiting components that were additional to Southern Rhodesia seemed logical. I had spent most of my time since I entered Africa in S. Rhodesia. Nyasaland and Northern Rhodesia beckoned.

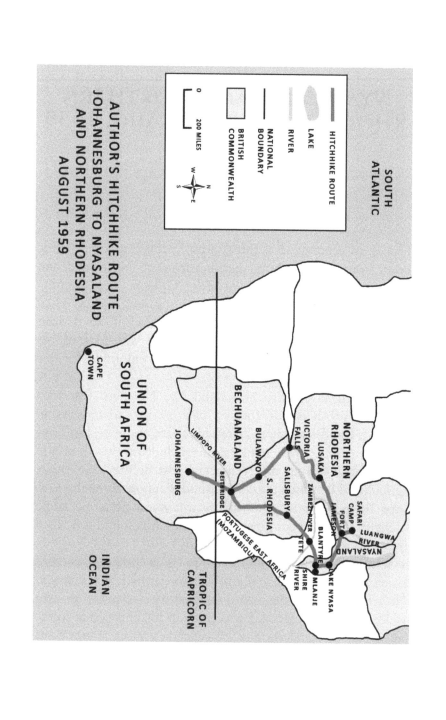

SOUTH
ATLANTIC

HITCHHIKE ROUTE

LAKE

RIVER

NATIONAL
BOUNDARY

BRITISH
COMMONWEALTH

0   200 MILES

AUTHOR'S HITCHHIKE ROUTE
JOHANNESBURG TO NYASALAND
AND NORTHERN RHODESIA
AUGUST 1959

CAPE
TOWN

UNION OF
SOUTH AFRICA

BECHUANALAND

JOHANNESBURG

LIMPOPO RIVER

BEITBRIDGE

BULAWAYO

S. RHODESIA

SALISBURY

PORTUGESE EAST AFRICA
(MOZAMBIQUA)

ZAMBEZI RIVER

TETE

VICTORIA
FALLS

LUSAKA

NORTHERN
RHODESIA

FORT
JAMESON

SAFARI
CAMP

LUANGWA
RIVER

NYASALAND

BLANTYRE

MLANJE

SHIRE
RIVER

LAKE NYASA

INDIAN
OCEAN

TROPIC OF
CAPRICORN

CHAPTER 11

LAND OF THE LAKE

Nyasaland on the horizon

On the northern outskirts of Johannesburg, which I had reached by bus, I soon got a lift in the direction of Southern Rhodesia. My driver was an affable Afrikaner farmer.

Jan said, "Man where do you come from?"

I exclaimed, "Joburg."

Jan smiled and scoffed, "With an accent like that you're not from South Africa."

For the umpteenth time I reminded my lifts I was from London.

Afrikaners were the typical landowners in the rural parts of the Union. They were people who the English-speaking South Africans should have respected because their farms were often a considerable distance from towns. They were greatly outnumbered by the natives living in the surrounding kraals.

Jan, my lift driver said, "I am puzzled that you don't want to go to the Kruger National Park but want to go further on.

I said, "Kruger needs a vehicle for viewing the wild animals. I want to go on a walking safari. I'm looking for a wilder area away from the majority of tourists."

Jan laughed, "I get you. That makes sense."

The open Highveld, with its vast fields of maize flew by and the road climbed a range of mountains known as the Soutpansberg. It then descended into the Lowveld. Here the bush crowded in from either side overtopped by the occasional huge baobab. I knew this type of country even though I had not been to the northern Transvaal before. It reminded me of the bush of the Rhodesian Sabi Valley where I had spent two years. The Lowveld of this part of South Africa was really a continuation of the Sabi Valley of Southern Rhodesia. It had similar scattered irrigation areas and ranches partially concealed by the ubiquitous bush. These farms were announced at the junction with the tarmac road that we were speeding along. Here a dirt track disappeared into the bush, no doubt accessing the farm buildings.

I was dropped by my farmer friend at Louis Trichardt. In no time, after brief refreshments I was on my way again and found myself back in Salisbury, Southern Rhodesia. Here I spent the night in the flat of one of my old mates from the Mount Hampden government employee's hostel. I had spent six months at this hostel while working in the Roads Department laboratory. Jim had moved on to better accommodation in the heart of the city.

Jim said with a sigh, "I wish I could come with you Peter, on your venture into the interior. Unfortunately I have used up all my leave."

In the morning I waited on the north-east outskirts of Salisbury on the road to Nyasaland. I was soon picked up by a slim, tall, suntanned man in his mid-twenties, driving a much mud splattered station wagon. His khaki attire made it clear he had a job in the open air.

Mike explained, "I am a Water Department technician employed by the Nyasaland Government. I am heading for Blantyre, the main town of Nyasaland. It was named after the locality in Scotland where David Livingstone lived. He was the great 19th-century missionary/explorer of the area we are about to travel across."

I found out later that Nyasaland has about the same area as Scotland, and about the same length as Great Britain (England, Scotland and Wales). It is a small country but long and narrow.

The road to Nyasaland, present-day Malawi, involved crossing into Mozambique, Portuguese East Africa, and later the Zambezi River. There was no bridge across this great river, which was particularly wide and fast flowing, so the road came to a halt at the bank.

We had been travelling through bush and scattered native cultivation in Mozambique up to this point. I could just see the buildings of some town on the opposite bank, which were several hundreds of yards away.

I noticed in the distance what appeared to be a large raft. It appeared to be attached to an overhead line which apparently stretched from one bank to the other. As the craft came nearer I saw it carried a battered lorry. The ferry eventually arrived at our side of the river.

Mike exclaimed, "It is about time they built a bridge. The Portuguese are unlikely to do that any time soon."

After the craft had been tethered Mike drove gingerly on to it. He chocked the wheels with some old timber he had in his station wagon. Mike gave an extra tug on the handbrake to make doubly sure he had minimised the chances of the vehicle slipping into the river. We both left the car as soon as this was done.

Mike said smiling, "We might stand a remote chance of surviving by swimming should we capsize. The crocs and giant fish with sharp teeth might dispute that. In the station wagon we have no hope should the raft be upturned by a wave!"

I said, "It is a case of being between the devil and the deep blue sea."

After a Land Rover had joined us at the back Mike exclaimed, "I felt the raft move!"

We were pulled across the River Zambezi by an old motor boat.

So we made our way towards the opposite bank. All the time we were menaced by the slopping of the waves at the margins of our floating bridge. Occasionally we aroused the curiosity of some indeterminate aquatic creatures of substantial

Crossing the River Zambezi. The author on a raft ferry pulled by a boat. Portuguese East Africa, July 1959.

size. These did not quite break the surface, but their presence was unmistakeable.

Tete was a small dusty town overlooking the River Zambezi where we disembarked after our river crossing.

On reaching Nyasaland, after Tete, we had to embark on another raft ferry in order to cross the River Shire. We were propelled by two stalwart blacks stripped to the waist, wet with sweat, pulling on a chain.

It was evening when we arrived in Blantyre.

Mike said, "You can sleep in my caravan tonight. You can doss down on the floor in yer sleeping bag."

I said spluttering, "I am more than pleased with your kind offer."

Ferry across the River Shire, a raft pulled manually.
Nyasaland, July1959.

Islamised native propelling ferry by pulling rope of raft.
Nyasaland, 1959.

We got on so well together. Being a weekend, Mike drove me to see the sights within striking distance of the town. We passed native cultivation where maize was prominent. Tea was grown on the slopes of the attractive mountainous area, often in European run plantations.

The climax of this excursion was the huge massif of Mlanje Mountain displaying sheer granite precipices. There were well wooded gullies with trees entangled with lianes. This reminded me of my expedition to the Vumba Mountains in Southern Rhodesia, with Roger from the government hostel in Salisbury. I fantasised that these subtropical forests were fragments of the elusive tropical rain forest but they were not low enough and therefore too cool for a steamy jungle. I never seemed to identify conclusively this type of forest. Short of reaching the Congo Basin of central Africa, I was never to be certain of finding this iconic vegetation. Mlanje is famous for its native cedar forest but much of this has been removed for timber. Mlanje was a giant of a mountain reaching about ten thousand feet. Mlanje welled up from the depths of the Earth's crust to cover hundreds of square miles. It was trapped in the south-east corner of Nyasaland by almost encircling foreign territory, Portuguese East Africa.

Dates and hot pursuit

On our way back to Blantyre Michael made a suggestion which fairly whetted my appetite.

He said, "I know two young ladies, in their late teens, daughters of tea plantation managers. These delectable damsels might be agreeable to accompanying us to the bioscope this evening."

I had to remind myself that bioscope was a southern African word for cinema.

I rejoined excitedly, "I like the cinema but it is much better with a young lady."

So racing back to town, a short phone call sealed our dates for the night.

Rona and Annette were two pretty girls, slim and leggy, with an indeterminate accent. You would therefore not know which country they were from. That is unless of course you met them in Nyasaland.

Mike and I met the girls outside the cinema, where their fathers had dropped them from the universal Land Rovers. These were characteristic of men wedded to the land.

Somehow I gyrated to the shorter of the two lovelies, Annette. The film was a romance but short of that I have only a hazy recollection. What was to follow was of much greater interest and consequently stands out in my memory in much greater clarity.

We had a coffee in a nearby cafe, an appropriate beverage in a region where the mild drug was once of value to the economy but has been supplanted by tea cultivation. We lingered over some liquor that the licensee pressed upon us. This was much to the excitement of the girls. Their cheeks were flushed even before they had downed the heart warming magic liquid. There is something enticing about a forbidden fruit that mother has said you must not sample.

Courting is a dangerous game, especially for girls, and especially when their escorts are not sincere. This is particularly the case when one of the escorts, me, just appears to be passing through. But more especially when he is from the wicked city of Joburg and heading for the back of beyond!

The event that was shortly to unfold was fraught with danger so as to make these uncertainties pale into insignificance.

One of the girls on suddenly glancing at her watch exclaimed, "We should be getting back!"

This was in a tone of voice that indicated meeting some sort of deadline. The concern expressed suggested something more than putting mother's mind at rest.

It should be remembered that this was long before mobile phones existed. Today people in general and the young in particular are constantly monitoring these gadgets in the street.

Surely the girls were not locked into some Cinderella fantasy where they had to be home before the stroke of midnight? Otherwise Mike's station wagon might be turned into a pumpkin, and Mike and I would be reduced to a goose and lizard respectively!

I knew the colonies were behind Britain in all sorts of ways. They were old fashioned. I was constantly reminded by the quaint customs and expressions of the white settlers in Africa. These harked back to a gentler age, which had gone in Britain. I glanced at my watch. It was 9:50pm. It had been dark for some time. The tropics are well known for darkness to descend early. As far as I was concerned the night was young. Then Mike made a similar exclamation as the girls. He leaped out of his chair, beckoning to the rest of us to do the same.

"We must get the girls home pronto! We must beat the deadline," he said.

Uninceremoniously he drew a note from his wallet, pristine and crisp, embellished with the Queen's head and the title "Federation of Rhodesia and Nyasaland." The currency of the Federation had not been in existence long. He slapped it down on the table. It was enough to pay for our refreshments and a generous tip, no doubt a compensation for our abrupt exit. I had no time to make my own contribution.

Mike, noticing the puzzled look on my face reminded me, "There is a curfew in the town and in the country at large. No vehicles and pedestrians are to be on the street after ten pm."

Such niceties did not seem to enter into my calculations when trekking through the "Dark Continent." Oversights of that nature, up to that time, had not unduly threatened me with disaster.

As we hurried to the car Mike said, "There is a state of emergency in Nyasaland. This applies especially in the towns and more particularly in the main town, Blantyre, which of course we are in." He further explained, as we travelled at breakneck speed through the deserted streets, "A hard-core of the natives is revolting. This is because of their dissatisfaction with white rule in general. They want Nyasaland to leave the Federation."

Three years after my adventure in Blantyre and environs Nyasaland had left the Federation as had Northern Rhodesia. The marriage of convenience that looked so promising in 1953, two years before I migrated to the country, was only to last ten years!

We continued our frenzied journey through the built-up area of Blantyre and Limbe. The two towns were close together and contained most of the Europeans in the country. This was a mere fraction of the white population of Southern Rhodesia. The Nyasaland whites were considerably more outnumbered by blacks than those in Southern Rhodesia.

I noticed Mike gazing in his mirror more frequently than he had previously. Straining my neck I caught sight of a smart looking Land Rover that appeared to be shadowing us. As we accelerated the distance between us did not diminish. Then suddenly we realised from a crescendo of horns, wails, and flashing lights, that we were being pursued not by terrorists but by the police!

Mike kept to the shadows and dimmed his lights. He did not want our pursuers to see his registration number. Mike knew the back streets. There was a terrifying squealing of brakes as he cornered. He apparently managed to shake off the police.

Mike exclaimed with glee, "Well that's got rid of the pigs."

Leaving the lights of the town behind, we continued our crazy dance up into the hills. We passed the serried ranks of tea bushes, just discernible in the faint moonlight. They were broken up by patches of forest. Then suddenly we entered the portals of a plantation house yard, and parked up in the shadows.

Mike and Rona remained behind while I escorted Annette to the big house, which appeared unlit on our side of the house. Groping around in the darkness I could just make out a settee in the lounge, on which we both flopped down. Unfortunately, our love making was too brief.

I effused, "Sorry Annette I must get back to Mike. He has to drop Rona at her family plantation."

"You're right," Annette whispered, not wanting to disturb the household, "that's ten miles away."

Kissing her I murmured, "I enjoyed your company."

I thought I could not encourage her more because Nyasaland was too far from Joburg to make regular courting trips. Besides I had other ambitions which would need great consideration.

Somehow Mike and I got back to his caravan, miraculously avoiding the attentions of the Federal Police. We were thoroughly drained by this hair-raising experience.

Temperature raised by nurses

I was on the road the next morning picked up by a tall, slim, faired-haired man, aged about thirty. He was clad in bush hat, khaki shorts and shirt, veldskoens (raw hide shoes) and long thick socks. This was typical attire of white males who spent much of their day in the open air.

James said proudly, "I am the manager of a tea estate close to Blantyre. We are on our way to a resort on the southern shore of Lake Nyasa."

James had an attractive, voluptuous young woman, apparently in her mid twenties, seated by the side of him. He beckoned me towards the back of the vehicle, where to my delight was another young lady of similar age but of more modest proportions.

My companion on the back seat said, "My name is Jean. My friend at the front is Joan. We are nurses at Blantyre Hospital. We are meeting colleagues later and making up a general swimming and frolicking party in the water and on the sands of Lake Nyasa."

I rejoined, "Jean, your frolicking party sounds exciting."

Nyasaland turned out to be the most attractive part of Africa I had seen. Everywhere it seemed there were forested hills, not the thick impenetrable unwelcoming kind. They were lightly wooded with a variety of tree species sporting leaves of different shades. In the valleys there was a patchwork of native fields. I suspected some had a rotation of cultivation in which fields would lie fallow for a time, when the forest would return. Occasionally more ambitious farms punctuated the bush, European owned plantations, which used the local native labour. It appeared an idyllic scene, but as I knew from the previous evening, everything was not always what it seemed.

We stopped at the side of the road, close to a village, where the Bantu natives were setting out craftwork. I selected a magnificently carved leopard in local polished wood, some nine inches long. The leopard was stretched out, as if perched on a rock. Its muscles seemed to ripple down its shoulders and flanks, as if to spring on some unwary prey. Built in and to the side of this skilful work was a semicircle with small bony white projections with an ivory consistency. This represented the setting sun. Under the whole thing, on the base, was the word Nyasaland, picked out in a similar material as the rays of the sun.

Jean said, "That's a nice carving you have got there. It has on it the emblem of Nyasaland."

We passed through Zomba, a small town with a distinct colonial air. Outside the governor's residence smartly turned out African ceremonial guards were standing to attention, their rifles and fixed bayonets well in evidence! These were not in the bland khaki uniforms of battle weary men, but colourfully turned out with fez head attire. Behind them fluttered the Union Jack, at the top of a high pole. There was no mistaking that Pax Britannica had been writ large over much of Africa. However, the word "Pax", peace, seemed inappropriate then. Zomba to the annoyance of much larger towns like Blantyre was the capital of Nyasaland.

A short distance outside Zomba we passed a platoon of African soldiers, this time dressed for business in khaki uniform and fully armed. They were marching by the side of the road led by a young white officer. This brought home to me the vulnerability of the whites, for here was a European depending on the loyalty of his men. They were divided not just by colour but an enormous gulf of culture, yet sharing a comradeship of belonging to the King's African Rifles!

James, our driver, said with fervour, "I only hope the KAR can keep the terrorists at bay!"

This fleeting scene, almost surreal, had a lasting impression on me. I remember mentioning it to a group of university students with whom I was sharing a class in Britain, after returning from Africa. I was a part-time student, while they were full time, significantly younger than me. They laughed about this example of "quaint" colonialism. We live in an increasingly cynical age where a growing number of people, particularly the young mock such institutions of the past. The acid test of this mockery is whether modern society is any better than what existed in yesteryears.

I wondered whether the ranks of native soldiers that had just passed us were more than an innocent exercise. Might it not have been a show of force to those black dissenters who might be lurking on the outskirts of the capital? The police chase in Blantyre, during a night curfew, might have been a curtain call to trouble further north in the direction we were moving. "There may be trouble ahead" was the song of the insurance advert on British television. Not two miles further down the road this belief was reinforced. We passed another group of native soldiers piling into the back of an army truck. Some of them were joking with each other. They seemed secure in the knowledge they had a paid job with a smart uniform and admiration from the general population. Clearly the dissenters among the public, the freedom fighters, did not share this view. It seemed that I escaped Rhodesia's National

Service just before disturbance from the restless indigenous people hotted up.

There is trouble ahead! King's African Rifles to stem any revolution. Nyasaland, 1959.

Lost World

Behind the capital was the Zomba Plateau. Nyasaland had more than one of these high, steep sided areas, relatively level on top.

I said with a chuckle, "The Zomba Plateau could be little visited. It could be a kind of lost world of the Conan Doyle type where one might expect creatures from another age. These might be dinosaur type monsters which have stood still in their evolution while the rest of the world has moved on."

This caused a huge amount of amusement.

We all murmured agreement when it was suggested by James, with a tone of sarcasm in his voice, "It would be good to park up. We could then climb the escarpment which the road has been following. It would be more than exciting to test Peter's theory that it is a lost world on top. The rest of the Lake Nyasa beach party will not be arriving until the next day. We have the best part of an afternoon to reach the lakeside resort a hundred miles away. This allows plenty of time to peek at prehistoric monsters."

At this they all burst out laughing.

We made sure we carried our water bottles with us. It took one hour of toil to ascend the two thousand foot high slope. This involved wending our way round the thorn bushes and msasa trees. A number of duiker and klipspringer antelopes were startled before we made the top.

On top of the Zomba Plateau. I amused my lift by imagining prehistoric monsters here. Nyasaland, 1959.

The view was stupendous, rocky hills, broke the bush to the east. A patchwork of native cultivation here and there scarcely interrupted the predominance of nature. It was distinctly cooler than the lowlands at the foot of the plateau. The plateau surface was far from uniform, but clearly less rugged than the scene to the east. Much of it was grassland with woody tracks disbursed across it. In the ravines was another world filled with a tangle of forest accompanied by ferns, mosses and lichens, almost a jungle. Here, the microclimate encouraged less evaporation. Therefore there was higher humidity than in the open.

Joan, the nurse, had accompanied her handsome plantation manager driver in the front passenger seat on our way to the "Lost World." She was rather attached to him. Joan would give him the "glad eye," always seeking his attention at any opportune moment. This happened when the vehicle had slowed down so we could admire a view. Most particularly it happened when we were climbing the "Lost World's" escarpment. Joan seemed to feign exhaustion from time to time, an excuse to stop and be comforted by the "apple of her eye."

"Please can we stop so I can get my breath back and rest my ankle which I have twisted," Joan would sob on more than one occasion.

To me and Jean, such amorous spectacles were a little trying. Jean and I did not seem to share the same romantic feelings. I believe she had a plantation manager in mind. She mentioned his name from time to time.

Disappointingly we did not find anything on the Zomba Plateau that was remotely comparable to Arthur Conan Doyle's "*Lost World.*" This was an adventure story set in the jungle of the Amazon basin of South America. The jungle concealed a huge mist shrouded plateau. Here the heroes of the story discovered a population of prehistoric monsters.

Frolics by the Lake

We covered the distance to the resort at the southern end of Lake Nyasa in no time. Lake Nyasa is no mean lake. It is one of the largest in Africa, which means it is numbered among the largest in the world. It is at least three times as wide as the narrowest part of the English Channel, from Dover to Calais, twenty miles multiplied by three. It is some three hundred miles in length. The lake occupied a quarter of the area of Nyasaland, hence the name of the country "The Land of the Lake."

To call Monkey Bay a resort was probably over the top. It had a modest collection of huts, but delightfully fashioned in the style of an African village. They were covered with thatched roofs and wooden walls, some round, rondavels. But of course they deferred to the tastes of the discerning Europeans, with ablutions that met modern standards. There were barbecue facilities if you wanted the fun of cooking yourself. Additionally the Monkey Bay resort had native catering staff for those who liked a more sedate experience.

The sun was setting when we sampled the refreshing waters of the lake. I dived under the waves, for the size of Lake Nyasa encouraged such sea like turbulence. This was a very welcome break from the heat and dust of my trek from Johannesburg.

In the morning I made up for the lack of light the previous evening, when we arrived, by promenading along the beach. This was enlivened by the sound and movement of the palm fronds as monkeys scampered through the trees. I could see there was a small forest clad island in the lake not far from the beach where I walked. It appeared to have a hut among the palm trees. Had a Man Friday been an occupant in the past?

An idyllic island in Lake Nyasa.

We were joined later in the morning by the rest of the anticipated beach party, planters from various parts of Nyasaland. The men were similar in appearance, tall, slim, physically fit, and in their mid-twenties to thirties, farm managers and the like. They were no doubt selected by their tea plantation companies because of their size and bearing. This was more likely to command respect from the native labour. The authority of Britain overseas had to be upheld. Some of the young white men by the lake were accompanied by their wives and girlfriends, but others looked footloose.

It was likely that some of the plantations were privately owned by a white family rather than a company who had a headquarters back in the UK. This might have meant that some of the men and women on the beach at Monkey Bay were owners of their Shangri-la plantations.

Sidling up to James who was chatting to Joan and Jean I said, "I have decided to cut loose from your exciting beach party. I don't want to out stay my welcome. Besides I want to explore Northern Rhodesia. It was extremely kind of you to give me a lift and share a wonderful climb with you all."

They all wished me well for the rest of my trip through Nyasaland and Northern Rhodesia.

One of the guests heard my conversation and said, "I am about to leave too, for the more northerly part of Nyasaland next to Northern Rhodesia. I am glad to give you a lift." Jeremy continued, "I will be passing through Lilongwe which is one hundred miles north of here."

I said excitedly, "I am more than pleased to accept your kind offer."

Lilongwe is now the capital of Malawi which superseded Nyasaland on independence and consequent black majority rule three years after my trek.

CHAPTER 12

NORTHERN RHODESIA PARADISE

Walk on the wild side

The beautiful, wooded, rugged, countryside of Nyasaland slipped by as we motored on. This was a country overlooked by European tourists, even those from southern Africa.

The highlight of my holiday experience, the three weeks I had taken off from my laboratory job in the dynamite factory in Johannesburg, was just around the corner. Indeed this was to be one of the most incredible moments of my whole African experience.

My lift driver Jeremy said, "I work as a manager on a plantation near the Northern Rhodesian border. I will drop you at Fort Jameson, a small town with few whites. It is beyond Lilongwe on the Northern Rhodesian road."

I was happy about that as I wanted to explore Southern Rhodesia's northern neighbour. I knew little about Northern Rhodesia other than what Mike had told me. Mike was my London school friend who visited me at the Sabi Valley Experiment Station, Southern Rhodesia, where I was working in the laboratory. My friend related his brother's experience on the Copperbelt of Northern Rhodesia. Mike visited me in Southern Rhodesia on his way to stay with his brother.

Fort Jameson did not seem to have anything that appealed to me. The first word of its name evoked a frontier community stemming from the turn of the century. These lands at that time were being wrested by the European pioneers from the Bantu. Indeed sixty years later, Fort Jameson still had the air of the frontier. This was not surprising as there was scarcely any settlement between it and Lusaka, the capital of Northern Rhodesia, two hundred miles to the west. I put up at a house advertising bed and breakfast, a modest residence not far from the centre of the dorp.

The morning saw me standing by the roadside on the western extremity of Fort Jameson. There was a squealing of brakes on my side of the road shortly after I had taken up my customary stance. A Volkswagen came to a halt just beyond me. I wasted no time in gathering up my rucksack and hurrying to the driver's window. The friendly face of a man in his late-twenties appeared.

In a South African accent he enquired, "Where are you heading?" He added immediately, "We are turning off the main road further on to go to the Luangwa Valley Game Reserve."

This information had an electrifying effect on me. I had hoped to visit that wild animal paradise.

I wasted no time in asking the driver, "Would you mind taking me there as my hitchhiking plans are flexible?"

He beckoned me to take a seat at the back.

He introduced himself, "My name is Jim Coetzee and my wife Wendy is sitting beside me."

Wendy was a pretty woman of moderate stature. Her husband was barely taller than her.

Mr and Mrs Coetzee were from Joburg. We compared notes on the merits of that city but agreed that it was great to get away from the concrete jungle.

Jim explained, "We have booked into the safari camp at Nsefu. This is close to the entrance to the southerly of the two game reserves in the Luangwa River Valley. This major river flows south into the Zambezi." Jim exclaimed with a grin, "I hope there will be room for you in the camp!"

Northern Rhodesia was a thinly populated country at that time, even by the blacks. Population was concentrated in the

Copperbelt on the northern fringe of the country and Lusaka the capital. The number of whites was small in comparison to the blacks, mainly located around the string of mines of the Copperbelt.

The Luangwa Valley was even more sparsely inhabited than much of the rural area of Northern Rhodesia, at least by humans. It was the reverse for wild animals. Some two hundred miles long and considerably lower than the plateau around it, which occupied much of the country. This caused the valley to be hot and dry.

We headed for the Nsefu Safari Camp along a dusty dirt road, with the customary jarring corrugations. This made me appreciate the tar of the main road we had just left.

The Luangwa Valley was infested with tsetse fly which caused sleeping sickness. Wild animals were immune to sleeping sickness. No doubt evolution had blessed them with a tolerance for it over aeons of time. Man, cattle and domestic animals were not immune. The Bantu and later the whites were comparatively new arrivals on much of the Southern African scene. They had not been long enough in the region to have immunity.

I explained, "The tsetse fly is good news for wild animals. It keeps development at bay. Cattle rearing, cultivation and settlement can't take place in tsetse fly areas. The tsetse fly is the friend of people like us providing we take precautions to avoid their bites. You need to keep yourself safe from their skin piercing attentions by insect repellent sprays and creams. Insect proof gauze on windows and a net over your bed is necessary. Travelling in the dry season is a great help, as we are doing, because insect attentions are at a minimum."

I hoped I did not sound too pompous in saying all this. However, they seemed appreciative of my words.

I elaborated, "I know something about the tsetse fly because I lived in an area of the Lowveld of Southern Rhodesia. Here there had been tsetse fly until the government killed all the wildlife. The wild animals carry the fly so killing wild animals eradicated the tsetse fly. This was done in a huge area covering more than one thousand square miles. This prevented cattle and humans dying from sleeping sickness in neighbouring areas. The spread of the fly was prevented"

These words caused Jim to exclaim, "Shame!"

Wendy added, "Terrible the wild animals had to be killed."

The bush slipped by, an assortment of trees, flat topped acacia, mopane, and thorn bushes. Dispersed between these were grasses that had long lost their feathery inflorescences and greenery. It was winter, when in spite of the name of that season it was baking hot by midday. Not a drop of rain had fallen for weeks.

We observed the bush on either side in the hope of seeing some spectacular wildlife. Even outside the game reserve proper this was still possible at that distance time. We were not successful. No self respecting wild animal, whatever its size and boldness would hang about by the roadside when it heard the clatter of a vehicle. The great cloud of dust generated by a car was an early warning to such wary creatures. This game sanctuary and its environs must have been one of the most remote in southern Africa. In consequence many of the secondary roads had not been metalled. Visitors must have been sparse consequently game had not got used to the wiles of the two legged intruders if they were in vehicles. It was different in the Kruger National Park in South Africa. Here cars were treated with indifference by the animal inmates provided they were driven slowly.

Jim suddenly informed me, "According to the brochure they posted to me vehicles are not allowed to tour around the Luangwa Game Reserve."

This raised the question in my mind as to how tourists were able to view the animals. He paused as if to give what was to follow more dramatic effect.

His earth shattering revelation was, "The wild animals: elephant, rhinoceros, buffalo, and leopard can be viewed up close and personal." This was followed by another pause, as if the following, as yet unnamed creature, needed even more respect, "And of course lion!" The punch line followed an even longer pause, "These, the most savage creatures on earth are viewed on foot in the wild!"

All this was too much for me to absorb in one go. This picture of game viewing, with all its inherent dangers, fired my imagination. I almost leapt out of the car's back seat with excitement.

I said, "I am absolutely gob smacked by what you are saying Jim!"

Wendy chipped in solemnly, "Peter, Have you neglected to take into consideration one vital point. There is no guarantee you will be able to find accommodation in the safari camp!"

"You are so right Wendy. If it turned out like that it would be shattering," I verged on sobbing. "What could be the most important component of my three-week venture into the interior of central Africa hinges on a place at the safari camp!"

I could hardly expect to share Tom and Wendy's hut. They were a young couple who apparently had not been married long. Should this happen I would become a true Cape gooseberry. This term I nearly called myself when I first shared the Devonshire Hill Hotel's dining room table in Cape Town with Ivan and Natty. They were apparently an item. This was when I was a student at Cape Town University prior to getting my lab technician post in Joburg.

It seemed for ever before we saw signs of a settlement. It was considerably more than the twenty miles of dirt road to the Sabi Valley Experiment Station, S. Rhodesia, from the tarred road. This was when I was working in a Rhodesian government laboratory prior to leaving for Cape Town.

No it was not a mirage, for the heat of the day can play tricks on you. A collection of rondavels, similar to round native like huts, could be seen before us.

To the side of the numbered rondavels was an elongated, low, thatched building. This announced on a plaque that it was the headquarters of the game reserve and visitor reception.

Jim and Wendy wandered over to the office, clutching their reservation tickets, with me in tow. I was crossing everything that I would be able to get accommodation, even my legs for I was dying for a pee.

A white official greeted us in khaki uniform emblazoned with a logo which announced he was the head ranger. Under this were the words "Northern Rhodesia Game Department." He allocated a hut to the Coetzees after stamping their reservation tickets and noting their passport numbers. They hung back to see what happened to me. I had gained a little Dutch courage, apologies to Afrikaners and the Dutch in southern Africa. This was because I had noticed the absence of any visitor's parked vehicles other than the Coetzees' car. There were a couple of Game Department Land Rovers parked nearby. I also observed there were half a dozen numbered huts which I assumed were for the use of tourists.

It had occurred to me that if there was no room at the inn I would be in dire straits. In the event of this I would have to throw myself on the mercy of the head ranger stood before me.

His hand moved in my direction followed by the words, "Reservation ticket," in a broad Afrikaans accent.

What could I do? To walk back to the tarmac would take at least a couple of days by which time I would be a dehydrated, shrivelled wreck. But before that it was more likely I would be ripped to pieces by some stray carnivore from the reserve. Alternatively I could be gorged and trampled by some irate large herbivore!

I spluttered in a contrite, feeble voice, "I have no reservation." Before he could reply I said "I have trekked some one thousand three hundred miles shouldering my rucksack. I have been caught up in a revolution in Nyasaland. Then I stumbled across the fabled Luangwa Valley. I understood this to be the best game viewing area in the whole of Africa. What is more I heard it has the best rangers."

This last sentence caused a smile to spread across the head ranger's face.

Laurens Van der Post, for that was the name on his desk, made an astounding claim.

"The Luangwa Valley is not only good for tourists armed with cameras, but also with a rifle. It has the best hunting in Africa. Hunters come from far and wide to shoot one of the big five." These were the iconic creatures that Jim had mentioned to me. The head ranger continued, "Controlled hunting under licence, in which American hunters featured large, could be had for a fee. This varied according to the animal selected. A successful clean shot by the tourist-hunter could be photographed with the hunter astride his trophy. An appropriate part of the dead animal's anatomy could be stuffed and mounted by a professional taxidermist!" The chief ranger added, "Hunting takes place in a distant part of the Luangwa Valley. The immediate vicinity of the safari camp, where we are standing, is for tourist photographic treks. These are on foot to view the game which could be as close as twenty yards. That is assuming the wind is in the right direction taking the scent of the viewers away from the animals!"

All this sounded incredible, beyond my wildest dreams. But it had not answered two vital questions on which the fulfilment of my fantasy depended. In the pause after this speech, it occurred to me that Mr Van der Post might not be concerned that I had no reservation.

He next spat out the word "passport" which I was quick to proffer. He made a note in his register followed up by, "How long would you like to stay?"

I nearly jumped for joy at this indirect announcement of acceptance of my request to stay at the camp.

At that moment I noticed the Coetzees. They had apparently been watching my encounter with the head ranger. Following this they had a huddled conversation for a few seconds. Before I could answer Laurens' question Jim stepped forward.

He said, "As my wife and I will be staying three days at the camp perhaps Peter could do the same. We could then give Peter a lift back to the tar!"

I squealed with delight, "All this is music to my ears. You have indeed become good mates, Jim and Wendy!"

Laurens smiled, "You, Mr Hardy, will be in hut two. Mr and Mrs Coetzee have been allocated hut one."

I did not therefore entirely become a Cape gooseberry as I did not share their hut!

Guide and Tracker

But there was one question that had not been answered. This determined whether my extreme adventure, on the threshold of which I was standing, came to a safe conclusion. I assumed the Coetzees knew the answer to this conundrum. I had seen, while we were travelling to the safari camp a brochure about the Luangwa Valley Game Reserves protruding from their glove compartment. They were better informed than me from this printed information.

On making the appropriate payment to Laurens I popped the burning question. "How could a pedestrian safari tourist safely observe a wild animal at close quarters? Squinting through the viewfinder of his camera he could be distracted from noticing the attentions of a bad tempered rhino or whatnot."

Laurens face lighted up at this pointed question as did the Coetzees standing close by. There is nothing that pleases a person of whatever age and station being asked a question by an innocent person of less than streetwise calibre.

Mr Van der Post put on his best head ranger pose. He said solemnly, "The walking party will assemble at the crack of dawn, when the rim of the sun has not quite peeked over the horizon. It will then be led into the bush by a very experienced armed African guide. He will be accompanied by an equally experienced black tracker, similarly armed with a powerful rifle. The black rangers are crack shots. They are provided for the protection of the safari party should any animals threaten its safety. The game viewers should be respectful to the animals, absolutely quiet, and follow the instruction of the guide conducted in signs and whispers." The head ranger added, "The object of the conducted foot exploration is to observe the wildlife in their natural state. They must not be disturbed and certainly not to be shot, except in dire circumstances. To have to kill an animal in the conservation area around the safari camp is a sign of failure. The viewing has gone wrong. The participants have not followed the guide's instructions to the letter!"

At this point I interjected, "How can the Game Department reconcile this benevolence, an admirable stance on conservation, but at the same time condone hunting?"

Mr Van der Post seemed a little uncomfortable with this question. He said defensively, "In some parts of the habitat the wild animals need to be thinned out. This is because their numbers could be too great for the environment to support. Elephants fall particularly into this category. When their population exceeds the carrying capacity of the land excessive damage is done to the habitat. Too many trees are pushed over to get at the more tasty shoots and berries, on the higher branches. Only selected animals are hunted, perhaps those showing age or infirmity. These are animals that made little contribution to the well-being of the herd. Hunting is a great source of income as licenses to shoot are very expensive. Only the wealthy can afford such luxuries. This income is ploughed back into conservation projects."

I felt I could counter this argument. Pointing out that a major reason why the animal numbers in the sanctuary became too great was because they were confined to a limited area. They were not allowed to spread beyond the game reserve. This was no doubt because they would come into conflict with human economic activity. However, I did not want to push this argument too far. It would not be right to antagonise Laurens. He had kindly found me accommodation at the safari camp at short notice.

Laurens said, "Dawn is one of the best times of the day for game viewing. Many animals are active at this the coolest time of the day. After a couple of hours the guests return to the camp for breakfast. They then return to the bush to absorb the general natural history of the place. Tree, and shrub recognition, spider activity and the like are all part of this. Late afternoon and evening are also times to observe wildlife going about its business."

We retired to our huts. As it was well into the afternoon I was glad there was nothing planned for the rest of the day. Although it was supposed to be the cooler winter season, the cloudless skies made the hours on either side of midday very warm indeed. This seemed exacerbated by the drought.

The only thing that I had to attend to was the evening meal, provided by the camps black staff. So I flopped on top of my bed. I did not even bother to open my rucksack and shoot the contents into the cupboard. I figured I could do that and attend to my toiletry in the ablutions block during the hour before the meal. Meanwhile I could lie in comfort on my back looking up at the inside of the thatched roof of my hut. The moving foliage of the acacia tree just outside my window provided added soothing distraction.

Mealtime in the African bush, especially in the cool of the evening, illuminated by a campfire, is always a magic moment. It binds the participants together with echoes of a primeval past when all humans were hunter gatherers, Bushmen. It was a simple meal. There were shreds of biltong, served with salad of bananas, paw-paws, corn on the cob and avocado pears. The black cook and servers were in attendance. It reminded me a bit like my life in the bachelors' mess of Southern Rhodesia, except our meals were on the stoep (porch).

Jim, Wendy and I were the only visitors at that time, as previous guests had left that morning. Our conversations were therefore less inhibited due to the absence of other whites. We had already got to know each other from our journey from Fort Jameson.

I said to Jim and Wendy, "It's good we are the only tourists at this time. We can concentrate on each other's company and not be distracted by other visitors."

In saying this I had to be careful not to catch Wendy's eye. She was attractive.

Wendy said, "That's right. I found the evening meal more than exciting with the fire crackling and a wonderful view of the starlit sky."

We then launched into exchanging our experiences in living in South Africa.

I said, "I am missing the beauty of Cape Town after an unforgettable year as a student there. But it is great to be earning again in Joburg."

Jim enthused, "Your experience sounds great. I am running a building business in that wicked city and finding plenty of work. Wendy is my secretary. She is very good at finding clients that want an individual character house built."

With this accolade Wendy chuckled.

Exhausting ourselves over such exchanges, suitably lubricated with beer, we wished each other, "Good night." On which note we returned to our huts, full of anticipation for the excitements that the following day should bring.

My hut had screens on the window and door, fine mesh that aimed to prevent the entry of insects. They could be of the biting kind, carriers of malaria and sleeping sickness. In spite of this I used the net provided, that hung over my bed. Fortunately it was the dry season so puddles had dried up and the Luangwa River's waters were at their lowest level. Breeding sites for insects that carried disease were at a minimum.

I did not get the sleep I should have had because the sounds of the African night came drifting through the window. There were low growls in the distance and the crunching of undergrowth from some prowler who was not intimidated by the dark. Additionally I was concerned that I might miss the early morning call for the crack of dawn game viewings.

The animals of the bush take the view that the "early bird catches the worm."

One thing on which my mind was easy was that I felt comfortable that no large animal could enter my hut. This was because of the thick stockade made of thorn bushes, reinforced by strands of barbed wire, which encircled the camp. Rather like the perimeter fence which surrounded some African villages (kraals), although minus barbed wire. However, at some unearthly hour I heard a loud knock on my door.

An African voice cried out, "We are about to assemble for the bush trip."

The previous evening I had laid out all that I needed for the expedition. Foremost of which was my water bottle, and two cameras. One was for taking black-and-white pictures of diminutive size, and the other large colour slides.

With mounting excitement the Coetzees and I joined the game guard, Abraham, a tall, lithe, khaki uniform clad Bantu in his 30s. Africans seem to be more difficult to age and many did not know their birth date. Unlike us whites Abraham had long trousers, a wise precaution in the bush because of thorns and other irritants that pierce the legs. The soberness of his khaki contrasted with the colourful check shirts that we wore. Mine and the Coetzees did not blend with the dull winter colours of the bush. Camouflage is a needful precaution when you are approaching a deadly adversary.

Jim said, "I think we are overdressed. Our colours are too bright. I only hope the animals don't notice!"

Abraham's most impressive attribute was not his appropriate dress but his rifle. It was more powerful than my .22 of the Sabi Valley. His rifle was a .303. It was not the heaviest calibre. However, fired in quick succession it could stop an irritable bull elephant or buffalo that might mean us harm.

Elijah was a small black man, but wiry, alert. He had a fine tuned concentration that comes of years of observing the signs of nature long after the animals have passed. This was the CV of a tracker.

Our party was small, five in total, but that made for a more manageable size as far as our leader Abraham was concerned. Additionally the tourist part of the party had an intense interest in the environment in spite of our city origins. Jim and Wendy had resisted the temptation of lounging on the gorgeous sandy beaches of the South African coast. This was the holiday Mecca of many whites resident in the Union.

The first glimmer of light appeared on the edge of the horizon. Abraham pointed to the bush which was still draped in intense shadows.

"Move quietly forward. Do not step on sticks. They make a noise!"

Abraham led the way with the Coetzees just behind him, followed by me. The tracker covered our rear. What we had just started might seem an act of great folly, entering the lion's den, so to speak. But to us and me in particular, it seemed a comfortable thing to do with the protection of our black guardians. They were no doubt products of service in the King's African Rifles in their youth. Disciplined men ready to take on terrorists who might have threatened the *Pax Britannica*. This was a useful introductory training for any black safari guide and tracker.

The herb layer beneath the well spaced acacia trees was easy to trample underfoot. The summer waist height grasses had died down and crumpled from the daytime heat of the dry season. No longer did they conceal reptiles. Any self-respecting snake, and the like, would not be around to snap at our ankles. They would be in suspended animation in some cleft or burrow in the ground. But in spite of this I had thick, tough, elasticated socks, extending half way up my legs. These helped to repel any skin piercing object of the natural world that was around in the drought.

CHAPTER 13

"Darkest Africa" realised

Up close and personal

Our walking safari in the Luangwa Game Reserve of Northern Rhodesia, now Zambia, was beginning to look serious. I kept close to my two companions from Johannesburg but more particularly close to the two black rangers armed with powerful rifles. I hoped we all remembered the Chief Ranger's words back at the camp.

"We must never speak a word on nearing wild animals."

The bush became clearer as we penetrated deeper, as the light of the rising sun did battle with the night.

The guide suddenly beckoned us to stop, his gun raised. Elijah, the tracker, came round to the front to join Abraham, his rifle at the ready. I was not exactly happy with this move as I had no one to cover me from the back. Anything could creep up on me in the twilight!

As I strained my eyes, all the time adjusting to the changing light I caught sight of an incredible array of massive animals. They were strung out before us, barely twenty yards away. Their outline became clearer as the light improved. They appeared to stand shoulder to shoulder almost across my whole field of vision. These huge cattle like beasts were arranged not just in one line but reinforced by line on line behind. They seemed to morph into a phalanx of fierce soldiers. They were staring at us from eyes set in huge heads.

These were armour plated by a massive bony structure erupting from their forehead. From this reinforcement great curved horns extended to the side.

They must have stood at least as high as I am tall, five feet five inches. Dark in hue so they almost merged with the shadows around them. As the light increased huge muscles were revealed in their shoulders, taunt as if contemplating flight or fight!

There must have been one hundred of them. Within a group of adults, more closely knit than the rest, was undoubtedly a family group. They had young. There was no mistaking the species, African buffalo. They were regarded by naturalists and hunters as the most dangerous of African mammals! They had a disturbing habit of laying in wait for any animal or human that annoyed them and more particularly wounded them. The young of our herd made them considerably more wary, unpredictable and consequently dangerous. Any second they could charge.

The fact that the light was poor, but getting better by the minute, meant that photography was difficult. How I had the nerve to wait until my camera clicked after a long exposure, I will never know. Every click of the camera shutter by Wendy and the whirling of Jim's cine camera were clearly registered by the animals. Their muscles seemed to respond with a shiver.

Our armed guardians levelled their rifles. They appeared to take aim as one massive bull. He was a step in front of the herd. He seemed to flex his muscles more than the rest. Then in one sudden movement the herd were off to our right. They were swallowed by the diminishing shadows of the bush. This was an incredible experience. The most exciting, up to that moment, of my life! If anything could personify the hair raising exhilarating feeling of authentic Africa, this was it. My white companions were equally moved by the moment. Our black guardians were clearly elated that we were blown away by the majesty of the scene we had just witnessed.

Breakfast was more than normally gulped down. The adrenaline rush, stimulated by the mixture of intense emotions generated by our recent experience, made hunger pangs even greater than usual.

Jim said, "Our buffalo encounter was the most exciting moment of my life."

Wendy interjected, "I thought our wedding day was that. You always used to say that in the months after our marriage."

I felt I should say something to smooth over this thorny issue. I could not think of anything diplomatic to say. After all I was only a hitchhiker that they had picked up. However, I was beginning to feel more like a Cape gooseberry, a person who joins a supposedly enamoured couple but is not really welcome. I had that feeling in Cape Town when I joined Ivan's and Natty's excursions.

Shit advertises sex

Within an hour or so we were off again, threading our way through the bush before the heat of midday overtook us. Elijah, the tracker, examined the ground from time to time, relaying in Shona to the guide what the clues indicated. Abraham would translate, for our benefit, into English.

He said, by way of summarising Elijah's interjections, "A broken twig, chewed leaves, footprints, type and freshness of dung, were things to look at."

Such spore was a mine of information to an expert and our black guardians were certainly that. They revealed the species, the size, condition and how recently the animal passed that spot.

One occasion excited the tracker. It caused Abraham, the guide, to quicken his step and our anticipation. Then with an inconspicuous gesture with his hand we stopped in our tracks and raised our eyes to the middle distance.

My lift companions and armed guide. The rhinoceros is
just a speck. Luangwa, N.Rhodesia, 1959.

In a clearing among the bushes and scattered trees was the
unmistakable silhouette of a lone rhinoceros. This large male
was apparently quite oblivious to our presence some forty
yards away. We tried to blend in as much as possible with a
thorn bush. This was somewhat laughable in view of the
colourful nature of our shirts. Thankfully for us rhinos have
poor eyesight, which was just as well as we stood there with
our trousers down, so to speak. They do not have the incredible
sight of the cats, lions of course included. Rhinos don't have
keen eyesight because they are not carnivores (meat eaters) but
herbivores (plant eaters). More especially they are browsers,
crunching at the shoots of any bush that took their fancy!
They are not on the menu of big carnivores. They are too
dangerous. Not having good eyesight does not matter to them.

Rhinos are massive animals, with formidable horns, fearless and bad tempered. Practically every other species gives them a wide berth. However, sight is one thing, smell and sound is another matter. Any whiff of sweaty tourists is noticed, particularly one like me who did not shower frequently because of the nature of my hitchhikes. We all hoped Abraham had taken note of which way the wind was blowing. There was the need for our scent to be carried away from this ugly beast. He appeared to be defecating. In fact rhino dung completely surrounded him in various states of freshness.

Apparently rhino, like many animals want to advertise their territory. How better than to mark it in a very smelly way? Their great turds do this job. Such business cards, excuse the pun, to another rhino contains a host of messages. It includes the degree of sexual maturity of a female, her readiness to mate. This is extremely important in finding a breeding partner across the vast distances of the great African wilderness!

Today in the third decade of the twenty first century there is fragmentation of the range of many species of animals, particularly in Africa. This results from poaching and destruction of habitats by agriculture with rising human population. It means that often an animal has to leave its fragment of habitat to reach another isolated piece. He has to trudge across inhospitable territory of farmland and human settlement, to find a mate! The chances of this are obviously much reduced.

The rhino is in a much more vulnerable position today because of the deliberate targeting of rhinos by poachers. It was announced in 2018 that the last male of the Northern White Rhino sub species had died. The two remaining females are the only hope of continuing the species if artificial insemination is successful from stored sperm.

Poachers are anxious to get a share of the astronomical price that rhino horn commands. This is largely driven by the demand from Southeast Asia, China in particular, for the products from rhino horn. The horn misguidedly fuels the belief that it has aphrodisiac properties. The continued expansion of the Chinese middle class means that there is a ready demand for rhino horn and the means to buy it.

Elephants are in a similar precarious position being slaughtered in their thousands every year by poachers, even in the national parks. Their ivory tusks largely arrive undercover in China. Here they are carved into ornaments of all kinds. They are used for personal adornment or as an embellishment to the sitting room shelf!

Since the retreat of West European influence in Africa, particularly in the former British colonies, the Chinese have largely filled the vacuum. This has happened in Northern Rhodesia, now Zambia, where I observed that incredible herd of buffalo and the lone rhino. The great engineering works the Chinese have fostered, including roads, railways and mines, has accelerated the development of Africa. The insatiable demand for minerals and other products has resulted in their shipment to feed the astronomical expansion of the Chinese economy. This does not necessarily benefit the local people of Africa. A host of Chinese technicians, engineers and managers have invaded Africa. It is difficult to visualise much of a future for such iconic animals as rhino and elephant with the advance of such a juggernaut.

We backed away from our rhino, taking advantage of the cover of the bushes. Then his attention was aroused by the snapping of a twig. This was when one of us put a foot wrong, usually a speciality of mine! He raised his head as if sampling the air for the slightest odour of something unusual. I half expected him to utter, "I smell the blood of an Englishman!" There was no time to wonder what he would do next. We crouched and crept our way round any scrap of vegetation that would give us cover. We were desperate to distance ourselves from a possible charge.

When we out distanced the rhino, Jim sighed with relief, "Thank god we got away from that brute."

Luangwa River

We found ourselves close to the bank of the Luangwa River, but concealed by a thorn bush.

The River Luangwa. Left to right, armed guide, lift driver, and author. Hippo in river. July 1959.

Abraham whispered, "This Is not the bank of the river now. It was only the bank when the river was in full flood. It has not been full of water for some months! We are in the dry season and the river has shrunk from where we are to the middle of the river."

This was well below where it must have been at the height of the rainy season. The river was now a mere trickle by comparison. But this trickle was enough to attract a variety of animals from the surrounding bush which were pulled by its life-giving water. Later we moved to the river bank when the coast was clear of danger.

Many water sources; pans, flei (marsh) and puddles scattered about the bush, had dried up. Pans had been ponds early in the dry season but had now lost their water. Evaporation turned them into encrustations of salt (sodium chloride). This mineral, vital to nutrition in limited quantities, was almost as necessary as water. The game of the African bush moved great distances to a salt lick.

From our concealed vantage point we had a grandstand view of the comings and goings of wild animals taking their fill by the edge of the water of the Luangwa River. There were the usual mixture of zebra and wildebeest with a lesser quantity of Thompson Gazelle. This was one of the more common antelope in southern Africa. But additionally there was a species of antelope of moderate size, whose coat seemed to catch the sun. This gave to it a brownish red hue.

Abraham, our leading ranger, said in a whisper, "Those antelopes are Puku. This part of Northern Rhodesia has more Puku antelope than anywhere else. This is the home of the species."

We made our way back to camp, Abraham and Elijah ever vigilant, clutching their rifles in a determined way. On a return journey one can fall into the error of being more relaxed. It is said more accidents happen on the way back.

On reaching the camp Wendy said, "That was another exciting day but I am glad to get back to the camp unmolested."

Jim followed, "You don't only have to watch your back in the bush but also in the concrete jungle of Joburg."

The evening meal under the night sky at Nsefu was a particularly memorable time.

I said, "It seems all the constellations of stars of the southern hemisphere are laid out above us."

Jim enthused, "In Joburg we don't see as many stars as we see here."

Wendy followed, "It's so romantic!"

At the safari camp illumination was by oil lamps strung at regular, but widely dispersed intervals. Many of these were out because much of the camp was empty of tourists. Light pollution was minimal and so did not detract from the star light.

We had the full attention of the black cook and serving staff and could take in the ambience of the place without the distraction of other game viewers.

The next day was to be our last at this immeasurably memorable spot.

Jim said, "I am very sad we are not staying longer in this magical place." Wendy and I murmured agreement.

We made our usual, very early, morning trek into the bush. Expectation was high that we might witness another natural spectacle. Single file, silence, and attendance to every detail of the terrain was the order of the day. Putting a foot wrong, thereby giving the game away was avoided. We searched our surroundings for anything that would indicate game of any description was near. True we had two black professional observers, one at the front and one following me closely at the back.

We were reminded by Laurens, the white chief ranger, when we first arrived at the reserve, "Ten eyes are better than four."

Wendy turning to me whispered, "It would be nice if we could see some insects."

I replied in hushed tones, "It's too dry for them."

Not to see humble invertebrates (animals without backbones) was a disappointment. Being the dry season such creatures were at a minimum. Forty years later I visited the Kruger National Park on a rare visit to South Africa. On a similar guided walkabout to Luangwa, because of occasional rain, invertebrates were active. There was a liberal sprinkling of these in the form of spiders, some that dwarfed those I was accustomed to in Britain. I collided with their webs strung across the path. This resulted in the huge eight legged creatures getting a lift on my chest!

Giants startle us

We reached an area at Luangwa that seemed more open than much of the savannah we had passed through. Trees had been toppled in some inexplicable way. There were great piles of dung, one lot piled on top of another. If it had been the wet season I would probably have seen dung beetles busily rolling marbles of the fetid material in which they had laid their eggs. A sight I witnessed in the Kruger all those years later. These turds were a welcome food supply for the emerging larvae of the dung beetle some time later.

Abraham waved his hand slightly to the left, a sure sign that we were to stop. Straining our eyes, we saw a small herd of dull coloured mammals emerge from the bush two hundred yards away. Objects which are far away can be difficult to size. You need to know their distance from you to do that with any certainty. But these creatures must have been enormous judging by their shoulder height against the neighbouring trees. In spite of the distance, two white elongated structures could be seen, one emerging from either side of where their mouths must have been. Strange to say we did not have any binoculars. In my case it would have been too heavy because I did not have my own personal transport.

With more careful observation of these huge animals at least one small animal of the same kind could be seen in front.

Abraham whispered, "The little elephant is being guided into position by the mother. The other adults, there are about ten, are forming a crescent. The ends of this are beginning to surround the mother and youngster."

This was clearly a defensive strategy. But why should they do that unless they got wind of us? I questioned Abraham about this later, well out of earshot of the elephants for they are very perceptive.

He said, "They probably did this because they were entering an area with few trees. They felt exposed."

Occasionally what must have been huge ears made gentle undulations. No mistaking it, this was a small family group of elephants and they were moving our way! Jim, Wendy and I got very excited at the prospect of seeing these giants close to.

Wendy exclaimed in a whisper, "Any chance of getting a picture up close and personal?"

Abraham turned his head and put a finger to his lips.

Cameras began to click, but they were still some distance away. I understood Jim and Wendy had telephoto lens incorporated in their still and cine cameras. This seemingly reduced the distance and magnified the objects of our interests. But I had no such attachment to my cameras, one for colour and the other black-and-white. At that moment it seemed ridiculous that I was not better equipped. I refer to my cameras!

In order to make up for not having a telephoto lens I would try to get one of my comrades, white or black, in the foreground of the picture. Apparently alongside the animal of my interest in the background but separated from them by a considerable distance. In this way, some idea of scale was gleaned. But no doubt the camera was confused. It would be trying to focus onto objects at widely differing distances. I got round this conundrum by adjusting the depth of focus, so scenes in the foreground were as sharp as those in the distance. The Coetzees cooperated greatly in this, by turning round to get themselves, at least partially, facing my camera. However, by doing this they had their backs facing the savage animals! They often had a nervous look on their faces. This was increased when the elephant, rhino or some other heavy weight advanced towards us.

Wendy seemed to cooperate more than she needed to. She seemed to be flattered that I wanted to take her picture as much as I wanted to photograph the elephant or other iconic creature. Perhaps she wanted to make her husband jealous! Some of these wild creatures, the animals I mean, were enormous close to. Yet they were positively ant like in many of my pictures. However, these photos were a dramatic record of my safari party. This particularly applied to the very professional appearance of our black guardians. They could be interpreted as dressed to kill, literally, with their rifles constantly at the ready.

The elephants continued to advance towards us, apparently oblivious of our presence. We were somewhat concealed by bushes and of course maintained silence, and made no obvious movements. Then something seemed to alert these juggernauts. What I assumed to be a bull elephant, had stepped slightly in front of the group. He was distinctly larger than the rest, his enormous ears flapping more determinedly than before. His head was raised in a defensive position. There was much trunk twitching as if sniffing the air in a more investigative way than previously. The ivory of the great tusks of this almost prehistoric looking creature glinted in the sunlight. He broke into a determined trot from what had been previously a confident amble.

It was obvious we had been detected and needed to take advantage of any cover available. The bush was quite open and judging from the occasional fallen tree this openness was due to elephant activity. This was confirmed some four decades later on a visit to see my daughter in South Africa. I saw an elephant in the Kruger National Park pushing over a tree and subsequently feed on the berries that were previously beyond his reach. I witnessed this on a similar walking safari as the one four decades earlier in Northern Rhodesia. Even in more developed South Africa, all those years later than my Luangwa Valley experience, it was possible to have a wilderness experience.

We managed to escape from the irate pachyderms (large, thick-skinned hoofed mammals) only by moving as silently as we could from one bush to another. The elephants particularly the mother, was no doubt in a heightened state of nervous tension because of the presence of a youngster.

On the way back to the camp we were rewarded by the iridescent colours of kingfishers and bee-eaters. They were darting from a river cliff in which they had excavated a number of nesting sites.

As we walked back to the camp Jim said, "We are returning to Fort Jameson this afternoon. As I said before I will drop you on the asphalt main road."

I beamed, "I cannot thank you enough for bringing me to this paradise. We have shared a spectacular experience. I intend to travel west towards Lusaka, the capital of Northern Rhodesia."

Treasure

We walked slowly towards the car park several yards from the camp. As this involved a three minute walk through the bush Abraham accompanied us, his rifle ever close to his side. We all had a downcast feeling at the thought of departing not only from this incredibly exciting place, but from our good companions, white and black.

Wendy wiped a tear, "I could cry at having to leave this wonderful spot."

Abraham suddenly pointed to a glittering creamy white object lying half hidden in the grass which had long crumpled and turned brown in the dry season. Picking it up, he showed it to each of us in turn. It was the end of an elephant's tusk, some twelve inches long and a good four inches in diameter at its widest point. The extremity, the business end of the tusk, was tapered and slightly turned up. The much wider other end was jagged. It had undoubtedly broken off from the main part of the tusk, presumably still remaining in the giant creature.

Abraham explained, "It was likely that the piece had snapped off when two bull elephants had clashed over territory or females. Their tusks had become locked together weakening one of the ivories."

One side of the ivory piece was extremely smooth, with hardly a blemish on it. The opposite side had a number of hairline cracks.

Abraham indicated, "This was because of the weather on this beautiful ivory. The hot and cold of summer and winter and day and night made it crack. It had two faces. One was looking up at the sun and moon and the other looking at the ground. The ground side was protected from the weather."

Ivory is so tough that it was difficult to imagine insect damage to it. Decomposes would have had a hard time reducing it to dust and returning it to the soil from which we all came. Weathering is a different matter. Stresses and strains are set up in whatever the material, even the most uncompromising of rocks. It was obvious that this substantial piece of ivory must have lain on the ground for a considerable amount of time. This explained the contrast between the two sides.

However, it seemed unlikely that this iconic object could have lain long in the position that Abraham found it that day. Surely staff and tourists walking from the camp to the car park would have spotted it long before. The dry season, when the incredibly tall grasses of summer had died down would have revealed it. It must have been moved from its original position. In spite of this logic I like to think it remains something of an enigma.

Jim said, "That object would make a wonderful souvenir for someone decorating a mantlepiece. It would result in a subject of much discussion with friends and family.

What was to follow was certainly more than surprising. Abraham returned the ivory to the place where it had been found, which we all witnessed. The Coetzees then walked a few steps forward, towards the car park. I always seemed to be following, after-all they deserved pride of place, as they had brought me to this magnificent spot!

Jim turned briefly and called out, "See you in the car Peter."

Jim turned again to face the car park. At this point Abraham darted to retrieve the ivory, in full view of me but apparently not the Coetzees. Pointing to a neighbouring tree he threw the tusk remnant at its foot. Here because of the shade the ground was practically free of an under-storey. Its position could not be clearer. Nodding to me it was obvious Abraham intended me to retrieve it. This was an easy task as the tree was on our route to the car park. There Jim and Wendy's Volkswagen could be clearly seen from the sunlight reflected from it. I was able to pick up the ivory and slip it into my rucksack without the Coetzees witnessing these shenanigans. Abraham and I exchanged knowing smiles.

This wonderful souvenir remains to this day one of my most treasured possessions. It has been an incredible prop for travel talks I have given over the years not only to students but adults as well. This natural artefact has a phallic appearance of astronomical proportions, particularly if wielded in particular ways. It raised wry smiles in practically everybody of whatever age and sex. If my talk fell flat, somewhat difficult when talking about the magic of Africa, my tusk did wonders to pep it up!

The way I acquired this treasure remains controversial. Apparently it was against the bye-laws of national parks and nature reserves generally for the public to take away any part of the environment. This even applies to urban parks as I know from working for a London parks department many years later. An individual was accosted by me for removing pebbles from a public open space in order to decorate his front garden! He was a hero from the Second World War, an internee of a Japanese prisoner of war camp. I had many an interesting conversation with him before and after his infringement of the park bye-laws about his war experiences. What he would have said if he had known I removed ivory from Africa I will never know!

If I had been affluent I could have obtained a hunting licence by paying out a fortune to the Federal Government. This was at the time of my Luangwa Valley adventure. I would no doubt have been able to take away a whole elephant's head complete with tusks. The hunting part of the Luangwa Valley would have enabled me to do this. Suitably stuffed and mounted on the wall it could have graced my home to impress my visitors. I could have regaled them with stories of darkest Africa and how brave I had been. So my very partial tusk seemed puny in comparison. But then I got it for free! On this latter point my conscience is not clear.

At the time I was in a quandary as to whether to tip Abraham. I had only a few seconds to decide. Otherwise Jim and Wendy would be wondering why I was hanging back with Abraham. If they had realised what was going on they might have felt they were more entitled to this magnificent trophy than me. After all they had brought me to this phenomenal place! However, if I'd paid Abraham it would be tantamount to him selling ivory. That was illegal in that part of the game reserve reserved for camera clicking tourists rather than trigger happy ones! Anyway, I could ill afford to give Abraham much money. To give him too little would have been an insult. I had plans in my mind for the use of my limited funds in the near future for a much greater adventure than hitherto!

CHAPTER 14

INCREDIBLE WATERS

On the road again

The corrugations and dust of the dirt road from the Luangwa
Game Reserve, Northern Rhodesia (now Zambia), became a
memory. We had arrived at the tarmac of the main road. As
promised, Jim and Wendy dropped me at the junction. I could
not thank them enough for the opportunity they gave me for
having one of the greatest experiences of my life! They had
given me a lift, transport wise and psychologically. We had
seen wildlife that sixty years later is on the brink of extinction.

I walked towards an extra large baobab tree by the roadside,
which seemed to afford more shade than most. There I could
wait in relative comfort for a lift west in the Lusaka direction. I
noticed that my rucksack had increased in weight. In it was the
beautifully carved wooden leopard I had bought in Nyasaland
(now Malawi). My wife threw it away in one of her cleaning
frenzies many years later! More particularly the ivory from the
Luangwa Valley was weighing me down, not to mention the
elephant's tooth that I also found in the reserve.

My lift came swifter than anticipated.

The driver was a white businessman, "Alec said, "I
commute regularly between Nyasaland and Lusaka."

The bush slipped by imperceptibly. Cultivation of maize
and tobacco, together with settlement became more noticeable
as we approached Lusaka.

I put up in a cheap hotel in the town, which like many in the Federation was laid out with wide geometrically arranged tree-lined streets. The more recently an overseas territory is developed by the British the more settlement's get away from the rambling street pattern of the Anglo-Saxons. Gill, the white hotel receptionist was intrigued by my rucksack. The straps were clearly biting into my shoulders and the whole thing was sagging over my buttocks. As I took it off Gill lifted it. The rucksack I mean not my buttocks.

"This is amazingly heavy! What have you got in it?"

"As I have come from Joburg what do you think?

She snapped back, "Gold bars I imagine!"

In the early morning I walked into the western suburbs of the town. The roads were lined with the well-to-do bungalows of European civil servants. This city was once, seven years earlier, the capital of Northern Rhodesia. The country was then a British colony quite separate from self governing Southern Rhodesia. At the time of my visit capital status had passed to Salisbury several hundred miles further south, in Southern Rhodesia. What I liked about the new bungalow district in Lusaka was the attempt to retain imposing native trees. Exotic sub tropical trees can flower magnificently, Jacarandas, flamboyants and the like. These grew especially well in the Federation. However, some native African trees had dignity, if not in colour then in form.

"The smoke that sounds"

It was not long before I got a lift from the universal businessman. The Federation had stimulated development of all kinds. This was not only in the more advanced economy of Southern Rhodesia but in its other two partners. Jack a man in his early forties, dressed as many European businessmen did in southern Africa in shorts. He was heading for Livingstone, a small town close to the Victoria Falls, a destination I could not wait to see.

Jack said, "This town used to be the capital of Northern Rhodesia until it was moved to Lusaka earlier in the century. I like having business in Livingstone. In my spare time I walk around the Falls. I never grow tired of the place."

I certainly did not tire of the Victoria Falls when I returned a few months later.

The vast majority of the towns in the area that was once the Federation have changed their names with the arrival of African majority rule. Livingstone town retained its British name. It was only some four miles away from the Falls. This place was named after the great missionary and explorer who shone a light on south central Africa. Livingstone was the first European to see the Falls in the middle of the nineteenth century. He named them after the great British Queen, head of the British Empire. Like Livingstone the Victoria Falls have retained their original British name. This I am sure is out of respect not only for Queen Victoria but also for Livingstone. The Portuguese appeared to have knowledge of the Falls before Livingstone but this seems to have been acquired indirectly, no doubt from natives.

It always seems to me somewhat arrogant to say that Europeans discover this and that geographical feature. Often the name they originally gave the object is retained for ever on a map. Not enough credence is given to native people. But discoveries have to be registered. They have to be written down and published. This was a technique over which Europeans had a monopoly. The Bantu inhabiting the area around the Victoria Falls called them *Mosi Oa Tunya*, "The smoke that sounds," at the time Livingstone arrived. This was because the spray and thunder of the Falls could be seen and heard some considerable distance away. I was determined to seek out the wondrous sight that I had heard about.

The next morning I exchanged banter with Carol, the receptionist.

Smiling I said, "I am going to walk to the Falls."

Carol retorted, "Mind your step some people have disappeared into its waters."

True to my word I wasted no time in walking to the Falls from my humble accommodation in Livingstone. As I drew nearer the spray and thunder seemed to come out of a hidden cleft in the ground. It was a kind of witch's cauldron concealed from the eyes of mortal men, which was being stirred vigorously. The "steam" from the brew was not consistent in its emissions but came out in spurts. I had taken the precaution of equipping myself with a raincoat. There was continual rain from the clouds of spray.

There was an increasing luxuriance of the vegetation on approaching the source of the spray and rumblings. This sudden eruption of greenery was in stark contrast to the dull browns of the savanna which surrounded it, typical of the dry season. This appeared as some additional miracle wrought by the witch. This oasis was appropriately called a rain forest. It was the product of the continual drenching, day and night, all through the year, by the spray from the Falls.

The rain forest of the Victoria Falls was only a few hundred yards wide, it extended for much of the one mile length of the Falls. It overlooked the great chasm into which the waters of the River Zambezi plunged three hundred feet onto the rocks below. Before I glimpsed the awesome spectacle of the Victoria Falls, I was conscious of the magical world of this rainforest. High trees were enveloped in creepers and lianas and festooned in places with lichens. Mosses were in abundance clinging to the trunks of the trees. Ferns covered the ground, and palms emerged above them. Mahogany and ebony were less frequent trees. The savanna above the Falls I heard contained elephant, buffalo, giraffe and zebra.

I met a Rhodesian man of similar age and small physique to me. John had hitchhiked from Salisbury.

He said, "The water volume pouring into the Falls' chasm varies depending on the season. The rainy season over the catchment area, the gathering ground of minor rivers and streams, feeds the headwaters of the Zambezi. This is on the plateau that is the Portuguese colony of Angola. It is joined later by other waterways. These swell the volume of the main river. From small beginnings the Zambezi becomes mighty!"

The huge amount of water cascading over the lip of the Falls was confined to a narrow gorge. This zigzagged for a number of miles from the maelstrom at the foot of the Falls. This gorge was largely concealed from the ground observer like the early discoverer Livingstone. It was only angels who could appreciate such miracles in their entirety. Later the wizardry of aircraft with cameras were able to do this. I had the good fortune later to do this myself from a light aircraft from which I took pictures.

In the dry season it was a different story. The water in the river had diminished at the time of my visit and consequently the volume of water of the Falls. Because of this the amount of spray generated by the Victoria Falls would vary at different times of the year. This would mean the rain forest by the Falls was likely to have different richness in its flora in different parts. This depended on the amount of exposure to spray throughout the year.

In spite of being called a rain forest this was but a fragment, certainly less than one square mile in area. I could not regard the Victoria Falls forest as an outlier of the true tropical rainforests. That was the elusive, iconic vegetation that I hoped to see. The Victoria Falls rain forest was situated on a plateau, some three thousand feet high. This no doubt modified the typical tropical rainforests of the equatorial African lowlands. The higher you go the cooler it gets.

The rain forest in spite of all its luxuriance was merely a screen for the natural wonder that lay a few feet away. I remembered Carol's words of warning at the hotel in Livingstone. I had to steady myself from slipping over the edge into the abyss below. Into this the thunderous waters toppled. Rocks at the bottom and on the cliff which formed the side of the cleft, into which the waters tumbled, seemed to rip the water apart. It turned it into a seething white mass disguising its watery consistency.

I had been viewing the Falls with my newly won Rhodesian friend John.

He informed me, "The Falls are not a continuous sheet of water but broken up into a number of cascades by islands of rock covered in rainforest. Each of these subsidiary falls are numbered among the largest to be seen anywhere in the world. Then as if not content to remain in the bottom of the cleft the waters sort a way of escape. The forces behind their turbulence are too great for confinement. They squeeze their mass through another section of the gorge at a sharp angle to the first. Each zigzag marks a former position of the Falls back in geological time. The further the zigzag is from the present Falls the older the former waterfalls is."

The river armed itself with a load of rocks which it had broken from its bed and sides. This constituted a stupendous hydraulic sandblasting tool and saw combined. It cut down its bed and hence created and deepened the gorge.

I viewed the Victoria Falls from my precarious position near the edge of the chasm. I could not see the full length of the Falls, some one mile in extent, only a segment of it. The portion I could see had to be multiplied several times to get a tentative measure of the immensity of this natural wonder.

The boiling waters and the green islands between were not the only spectacles that were painted on the mind's canvas. Arcing over this picture was a giant rainbow which wreathed backwards and forwards, up and down. It seemed the sun was attempting to paint a better scene than the previous one. In one instance a great rainbow did not just arc over the water but its' end reached the land close to where I was standing. Sidestepping a few paces I enveloped myself in a spectrum of colour. A neighbouring tourist agreed to take a picture of me with my camera, the one that took large colour slides. Selfy, a modern photographic method for taking you and the object of your desire, were not available then. Later I got this printed in a large format, an image of yours truly, the "crock of gold at the end of the rainbow!" The same tourist kindly lent me his raincoat. I had a colour picture taken with me on the brink of the chasm into which the Falls leapt, without getting wet from the spray.

The author enveloped by a rainbow at the Victoria Falls. Northern & Southern Rhodesia, 1959.

Author at Victoria Falls, Rhodesias. July 1959.

Perched close to the precipice in front of the Falls was more than a life-size statue of David Livingstone. The intrepid discoverer of the leaping waters in the middle of Africa saw them in 1855. This discovery was just over hundred years since I first set my eyes on this wonder. Clearly Livingstone had to endure privations that I could only imagine. He had no cool rondavel with mod cons and black servants to administer to his every need, as I experienced close by in the Luangwa Valley.

No doubt today, more than sixty years since my experience, the facilities for tourists are even more elaborate. This is in spite of the privations caused by Mugabe on the country south of the Falls. This is now Zimbabwe, formerly Southern Rhodesia. Tourists are often mollycoddled even in the most repressive regimes. They are not entirely aware of the suffering of the indigenous population around them. My accommodation then would now be regarded as positively primitive!

The statue of Livingstone depicted him in his expedition gear. Prominent was a hat which had a cloth drape attached to the back. This protected his neck from the ravages of the sun and insects.

There was a huge iron girder suspension bridge, which spanned the gorge. Here the Zambezi was confined hundreds of feet below, screaming out its wrath at being caged in such a narrow channel. Occasionally a train, car or commercial vehicle would venture across this tenuous connection between Southern and Northern Rhodesia. I nervously trod the boards at the side of the railway track and road.

A Passenger in a passing car shouted out, "Mind you don't fall."

They seemed to expect me to disappear into the raging torrent below through the crack of a missing timber. Such a fall would result in being torn to pieces by the sharp rocks below. This would be convenient for any cruising crocodile to devour lower down the river without getting indigestion! The iconic bridge is a favourite depiction on the stamps of Southern

The combined railway and road bridge at Victoria Falls.

Rhodesia, notably to celebrate the coronation of George VI in 1937.

There was a tastefully designed hotel near the Falls on the Southern Rhodesia side. It was not too obtrusive to detract from the impact of the Falls at the time of my visit. The city fathers of the Rhodesia's had good taste, so controlled development. An extensive natural buffer was left between the Falls and any neighbouring settlements of which Livingstone was the most notable. Sadly this is not the case with the Niagara Falls. This is another great waterfall of world stature on the border between the USA and Canada. I saw the Niagara Falls some fifty years later with my wife.

A flight of fancy

Observing the Victoria Falls from the ground did not do it justice. I had to take a flight to see its full extent. I heard there were light aircraft taking tourists for spins over the Victoria Falls. So I made my way to a small airfield close to the Falls used only by light aircraft. Here I had heard views could be had that only those with a head for heights could endure. Only angels had the priviledge of looking down on the earth before the age of flight.

An official said, "Sorry all the earlier flights are booked. I will reserve you a later flight."

By neglecting to catch an earlier plane when I took my flight of fancy over the Falls caused my photographs to pay dearly from the glare.

The plane I found myself in, at the Victoria Falls, accommodated only about eight passengers. It was similar to the De Havilland Rapide that visited us every few weeks at the Sabi Valley Agricultural Experiment Station in Southern Rhodesia. I skipped my laboratory duties at Sabi for a couple of hours to have a joy ride in the plane. I successfully took a number of photos of the Experiment Station from the plane. These included a very close encounter with the bachelors' mess bungalow which I shared with my colleagues, including the officer in charge of the Experiment Station. He replaced the permanent head officer who had disappeared without notice!

A De Havilland Rapide was a biplane, a double winged job joined by cross wires. This was a real pioneer of the African bush, capable of landing and taking off from short grass airstrips, hacked out of the wooded savanna. The days of early flight were echoed when taking to the air. It was more than an exciting affair. It involved a "wing and a prayer!" You almost expected to be presented with your pilot's wings for just being a passenger. The pilot at the Victoria Falls airstrip had a handlebar moustache, which he twitched from time to time. He looked every inch an ex RAF man.

"Make sure you are strapped in properly. It's going to be a hairy ride," he said expressively.

Flying over the Falls was truly spectacular. The spray appeared like smoke, now clearly not confined to a narrow strip of a few hundred yards that could be seen when viewed from the ground. The whole cleft into which the waters tumbled was visible, "smoking" away as if on fire. It was a mile or more in length. The broad width of the Zambezi River could be seen approaching the brink of the abyss. Shadows cast by the cliff filled it. As the plane banked to allow us a better view of this huge kloof from another angle, the sun illuminated the opposite wall. In the light of more recent astronomical discoveries, it was like a black hole pulling whole stars and planets down a giant plughole.

The Falls pulled whole trees that had probably floated down the river for some miles. These were perhaps pushed over by some giant at the water's edge. An elephant was anxious to consume the fruit and younger shoots that grew on it, out of reach of most other animals of the bush. Branches, sometimes whole trees, seemed to make a late effort to catch on to a rock. A last chance before they were swept over the brink into the raging maelstrom.

Stan, a middle aged, squat American passenger was strapped in by my side. He said excitably, "You can see from our high vantage point that the river is punctuated by islands. Some are of several acres. They are covered with richer and greener vegetation than the bush that surrounds the river. Gee I can see palm trees!"

Mammals of the bush, among them antelope, the big five, (elephants, rhino, buffalo, lions and leopards) jackals and the elusive wild dog, did not frequent the river's edge too near to the Falls. The quickening waters were enough to suggest to them that there was danger nearby. The vortices would have swept them up like some giant vacuum cleaner.

How did the aquatic life manage? Some fish must have found themselves hurtling over the brink to be dashed on the rocks below. But the more slippery characters among them, after the shakeup of their lives, "picked themselves up and dusted themselves down." They found themselves in the new world of the canyon!

From our biplane we viewed this stupendous channel cut down over eons of time into the rock. Not content to be straight and narrow, it described huge zigzags, each stretch between bends about one mile in length. It marked the position of former waterfalls, comparable to the one we had just passed over.

The pilot shouted above the engine's roar, "The zigzags of the Falls' gorge follow weaknesses in the Earth's crust, a crack, a geological fault. The river takes advantage of this."

Stan revealed his professorial and philosophical turn of mind, "Here is an indelible record of a landscape that was witnessed by the ancestors of modern man. Stone Age remains of prehistoric man have been found in proximity to the gorge. He was surrounded by strange wild animals that are now extinct. This makes written history of modern man puny, almost irrelevant. Here historical geology and palaeontology, the study of fossils, takes over."

Midday was just around the corner. This meant there was a substantial glare. Ground view was not as crisp as early in the morning. The sun was close to its highest point in the sky.

The Victoria Falls from the air must have been the top of any travelling photographer's dream who ventured into these parts. Because of the glare my attempt at photography was therefore a bit of a flop. I had two cameras with me, one for colour and the other for black-and-white. I soon realised when the plane did its gyrations over the Falls, that there was no time to switch from one to the other. I therefore opted to take all my aerial photos in black-and-white.

The haze won the day. I had hoped for an iconic picture of the "Smoke That Sounds." Many of my aerial snap shots of the Zambezi, tumbling into the underworld, were clouded by the shimmering haze generated by the sun. The radiation from the heated land must have been a major factor in the indistinctness of my photos. Any truly professional photographer would have had a filter attached to the camera's lens which would have taken care of the problem. I did not have such an embellishment! However, more by luck than judgement I got one or two reasonable shots when the plane banked in a particular way.

I regarded my attempts at photography, at least at that time, as record-keeping. It was a means of reminding me of the details of my ventures into the interior of Africa. "A picture is better than a thousand words", so they say. Some would say this is a good excuse for not writing an account of one's travels. It's all revealed in a photo album particularly one that is annotated, a scientific way of painting a picture. Occasionally, more by accident than design, my photographs of Africa have done credit to the subject I was taking.

King Coal's days are numbered

I was bowled over by the Victoria Falls. It took me some time to gather my thoughts about making my way back to Johannesburg and my job in particular. So I was back on the road again thumbing my way south-east towards Bulawayo. Trevor, an engineer who serviced the hydro electric power station at the Victoria Falls gave me a lift.

He asked me, "Where have you been." When I outlined my journey he said, "The way things are going you might have difficulty in repeating that journey in future!"

I asked him, "What do you mean?"

Trevor elaborated, "There seems to be unrest all over Africa and I think it's coming our way."

I replied "Funny you say that but in Nyasaland there was a night curfew, police patrols and a lot of army activity." Our vehicle was chased by the Federal police for being out at night during the curfew. Fortunately, we managed to shake them off in the streets of Blantyre. Our girlfriends of the evening enjoyed the bioscope (cinema) but were terrified by the police chase. My friend and I managed to deliver them to the safety of their tea plantation homes where their fathers were managers.

The road passed through the small industrial town of Wankie! This place changed its name, no doubt much to the relief of its citizens! It happened two decades later when Southern Rhodesia became Zimbabwe. On the outskirts of Wankie, but fortunately away from the road, was one of the most important coal mining areas in Southern Africa. Truckloads of the black stuff constantly passed along the railway running parallel to the road I travelled along. This happened thankfully some thirty miles west of it. The coal was on its way to the coal fired power stations of the main centres of population in Southern Rhodesia.

Trevor said proudly, "Hydro electric power is much cleaner than using coal. No air pollution is produced. When the electric power from the Kariba Dam comes on tap it should greatly help in toppling King Coal's nasty ways. Africa has tremendous potential for hydro electric power, greater than any other continent. However, there are changes in the amount of water between the wet and dry season. The quantity of power that might be generated therefore varies during the year."

More pleasantly we later skirted the largest national park in Southern Rhodesia. Sensibly the wild animals kept well away from the main road.

From Bulawayo I continued southwards to Beit Bridge. This bridge was named after a great benefactor of southern Africa. It was the main road crossing point of the Limpopo River from Southern Rhodesia into South Africa. I passed over the great steel structure, and gazed into the "greasy" Limpopo. I wondered whether my friend Colin from my Rhodesian civil service days was still performing his duties at the border as an immigration officer.

Louis Trichardt, the dorp at the foot of the Soutpansberg Mountains, was almost a blur as my lift sped on. We climbed through the Middleveld to the Highveld of the Transvaal. The temperature fell miraculously. I was reminded by this transect of South Africa's Northern climatic zones that I had completed a giant circle. I was back on the road I started on in my three-week trek through south-central Africa.

I reached Joburg later that day. The brown fumes of nitrogen dioxide heralded the Modderfontein industrial complex where I worked. I had completed a journey of some two thousand seven hundred miles on my annual three-week holiday from the dynamite factory!

I showed my large format colour slides to my colleagues in the central laboratory.

Marjory, a senior technician, said, "I find it difficult to believe you made such an adventurous journey in three weeks."

This was echoed by other technicians who saw my slides.

Marjory continued, "But who is the striking lady who keeps popping up in your pictures?"

"She is a married woman I bumped into among the wild animals!"

At this they all laughed.

Marjory rejoined, "Lounging on the beach at Durban or Cape Town in sight of the Indian and Atlantic Oceans is more to my liking!"

CHAPTER 15

COUNTING THE DAYS IN JOBURG

Scheming with a new friend

I joined the South African Youth Hostel Association club in central Johannesburg. I had been youth hostelling in Britain before leaving for Africa. Much of Britain was covered by my bicycle. I would stay overnight at hostels strategically placed in areas of natural beauty. This was done sometimes on my own but also with school friends and included ventures deep into the European continent. The YHA was truly international.

Cycling in Southern Africa for whites was not a serious option due to the vast distances. Many areas did not have a variety of scenery. There were an insufficient number of suitable accommodation and refreshment places at regular intervals. However, I had a bicycle while living in Cape Town but this was used locally.

Africans in Southern Africa were keen cyclists. They did not use their bicycles much on the roads. The multitude of paths which penetrated the bush linked Bantu villages. These were the native's highways.

The YHA club in central Joburg catered for people like me who were interested in the great out-doors. They had a minibus which covered much greater distances than any bicycle could. It deposited us at a South African youth hostel or a camp site where none was available.

Joburg Youth Hostel Club excursion. Eastern Transvaal
Province, S. Africa, 1959.

Patience is a virtue. Eastern Transvaal.

From the YHA clubhouse, for a minimum charge, men and women in their twenties, thirties and a little older travelled into the eastern Transvaal. We were carried as far as the weekend would allow. The minibus covered distances of two hundred miles or more and still allowed enough time for hiking. The area we visited was east of Johannesburg. It was a much more rugged area than that immediately around Joburg which was a type of prairie with wide fields of maize, the High Veld.

There were natural pools where we could cool down.
Eastern Transvaal.

Great chasms skirted the road. The author on the edge.
Eastern Transvaal, South Africa, 1959.

Not exactly youths! A stop on the way to a Youth Hostel,
Eastern Transvaal.

The eastern Transvaal, that part east of Johannesburg and its satellites, was a land of kloofs (ravines) and rocky hillsides. These were sanctuaries for natural woodland and wildlife. The smoother mountain slopes above were often clothed in plantations of pine, wattle and other fast growing non indigenous trees. They could provide timber, pulp and tannin, the latter for treating leather. The higher ground encouraged more rainfall suitable for the growth of forests. These plantations had more in common with Australia because of eucalyptus tree species introduced from there.

The youth hostels were often ramshackle establishments which had seen better days. Probably used originally as a precious mineral prospector's abode or shepherd's bothy. This was before the pastures were taken over by the serried ranks of non indigenous wattle and pine tree species. We would venture out into the clear air with wide vistas of rolling hills. All this was a welcome change from the crowded conurbation of Joburg, the Witwatersrand, where a sixth of the population of South Africa lived.

Youth Hostel, no mod cons, eastern Transvaal.

My potential hitchhike mate, Dave (left with the author).

There was a kitchen but you had to do your own cooking in South African youth hostels, unlike the British ones. There were male and female dormitories. Whites only used the hostels. A sheet sleeping bag you provided yourself, reinforced by the hostel's blankets.

I struck up a friendship with one particular guy. David was substantially bigger than me, approaching six feet, hefty, swarthy, and of Middle Eastern appearance. David was brought up in Britain, but had migrated to South Africa some years previously as had apparently a number of Jews.

David told me, "I am in the rag trade."

I said rather insensitively, "What on earth is that?"

"It is work to do with clothing. Tailoring has a lot to do with it. This is an important activity in Joburg," Dave said proudly.

Jews were also attracted to the Witwatersrand because of its association with precious metals and diamonds. Jews have long been connected with the jewellery trade.

David's origins were more complicated than his British nationality suggested.

He said, "My parents were Polish Jews."

Central and Eastern Europe and Poland in particular had one of the largest populations of Jews outside of the Middle East. This was the result of the Diaspora whereby Jews had, since time immemorial, sought their fortunes beyond their ancestral home. More particularly migration was a means of preserving their lives. Their homeland on the shores of the Eastern Mediterranean had always been a place of threats. Poland therefore contained some of the most prominent German concentration and extermination camps in the whole of Europe during the Second World War. Their inmates were predominantly Jews.

I had a hate/love complex towards British National Service. Moving to Africa, initially to Southern Rhodesia, meant compulsory two year British military service was delayed.

I was more than envious, however contradictory, when David said proudly, "I did my bit in the Royal Air Force!"

The mother of all adventures is hatched

My conversation with David turned to a possible teaming up on an expedition.

Dave said, "This would be far more ambitious than penetrating the lands east of Joburg." So protracted would this trek be into the interior of Africa that it would go well beyond my serendipitous wanderings to date.

I enthused, "This mother of all explorations would mean sacrificing our jobs, for no paid holiday period could encompass it."

Dave rejoined, "This trek requires great consideration." We agreed to discuss it further at a future date.

Our venture into the interior of Africa could wet the lips of even Stanley, Livingstone and the other great explorers of the "Dark Continent." That is if they could turn in their graves!

Dave and I met again on one of the YHA mini bus weekend trips to the Eastern Transvaal. When the hostellers had retired to the dormitories of the youth hostel, Dave and I discussed further our projected trek. I had bought two maps that covered the whole of the African continent. My understanding was that we were going to make a stab at crossing the whole African continent. I noticed Dave was particularly interested in the map that covered the African continent south of the equator. He only gave the northern half of Africa a cursory glance. At the time I did not give much thought to this.

Dave was at an advantage as he had visited Kenya, a British colony close to the equator, which was on our projected route. This was evidenced by his superb blow up pictures in black and white of Masai women, bare to their waists, inside their native village. What amazed me was the variability of the breasts of these ladies. There were every permutation of size and firmness. A sad sight was the elderly women had breasts which were reduced to mere flaps of skin. His close-ups of elephants demolishing Acacia trees were equally stunning but less erotic.

"I can't wait to see these wonders," I said excitedly.

We had valuable information from one of the regular youth hostellers who attended the YHA club in Johannesburg. Grant was a tall, lithe, hippy looking character in his thirties.

He hinted at seeing, "An incredible volcanic crater. This was long inactive. It was several miles across and was full of wild animals. This great hole in the ground was not far from Kilimanjaro, Africa's fabled snow capped mountain, a dormant volcano close to the equator."

I retorted excitedly, "That really whets my appetite."

All this information reinforced my earnestness to reach the region. By all accounts this area eclipsed the landscape and wildlife of southern Africa. However, Grant's appearance and casual manner somewhat put me off. Somehow, I felt he did not match my ideal of an African adventurer. I had to check myself here and examine my prejudices! I could not expect every "explorer," traveller is a better word, at that time, to be in the mould of the great adventurers of history. I could not be too haughty for most of Dave's and my projected route had been traversed by whites before, although probably in small numbers.

A different class of individual was beginning to venture into remote parts of the world. This was to be expected as travel became more efficient and faster. The spread of roads with moderate to good surfaces even in that far off time was a major factor. I was numbered among those modest individuals.

In spite of his apparently humble background and vocation Dave seemed to suggest a more refined side, almost cultured. Perhaps the RAF, considered the gentlemanly of the three British military services, had given him the edge in this respect. As I later found out many ladies apparently endorsed this opinion I had of him. He was a ladies' man.

Dave and I decided to embark on our Africa-Europe overland trek back to the UK as soon as possible. The cheapest means of travel would be used, including hitch-hiking, which we had both experienced under African conditions.

Dave said with conviction, "We could travel as far as Nairobi in Kenya, halfway across Africa, by hitch-hiking. This would be entirely through British territories with main roads, passable to motorised traffic, at least in the dry season. English was widely understood in these countries after years of British colonialism. They were stable under the peace brought by Britain." I thought Dave had painted too rosy a picture but I did not contradict him.

Apparently Dave enjoyed several years of living and working in Joburg.

He said emotionally, "I have built up a network of Jewish friends. I am not religious so I have gentile friends as well. But I feel isolated from the British way of life and London in particular."

When I said, "My parents and two teenage sisters still live together in London," Dave seemed envious. I continued, "I left for Africa four and a half years ago. It is about time I went back home. But will they nab me for Her Majesty's forces?" Dave laughed.

"I have no family!" Dave replied rather downcast.

It seemed that Dave's parents had left Poland for Britain in the 1930s. The increasing hostility of Central and East European people towards the Jewish minority caused this.

I found Dave had no difficulty in making new friends, male and female. His easy-going relaxed manner clearly had a major part to play in this. In many ways I was opposite to him and in consequence did not find making friends as easy as Dave.

Light at the end of the educational tunnel

The driving force of my urge to return to Britain was to gain a University degree. But there was more to it than that. I had a curiosity, particularly in the interaction of humans with their environment. The conversion of the natural world to urban and rural land uses troubled me. In short I was interested in geography. This would not just be satisfied with a qualification but preferably maintained as a lifelong interest! It was clear to me that Johannesburg was unlikely to fulfil these interests through academic study while I worked at the same time.

African Explosives had an advanced attitude to employee welfare. It seemed ahead of its time. The company had a section, which I assumed was an offshoot of the Personnel Department, which appeared to offer educational advice.

I approached this section and as luck would have it I was interviewed by a middle-aged thick- set man who was extremely knowledgeable and understanding.

Mr Mailer suggested, "Your best course of action is to return to the UK and try to take a degree course at Birkbeck College. This is an integral part of London University but especially geared for students who work full-time. By attending evening classes at this college you can gain a degree of the University as an internal student."

Gold mining evident

One day I decided to pay the Blackwells, friends of my father's sister another visit. I last visited them some two years previously when I was on my hitch-hike from Rhodesia to Cape Town University. Dorothy and Fred were pleased to see me at their bungalow in Benoni, a town close to Joburg. After we had tea, Fred offered to accompany me to Joburg on the suburban railway. He had to pay a visit to his place of work at the technical college. The train could have been on one of London's suburban circuits, which did not form part of the London Transport's underground complex. The Witwatersrand conurbation did not have a system comparable to the London Underground.

The passengers seemed just as earnest in their demeanour as those on similar transport in London. This was no doubt an occupational hazard of everyone, worldwide, on their way to and from their place of work. They were not lightly dressed as might be expected from it being South Africa. The high

A typical couple and their home in extended Johannesburg, Benoni.

altitude of Joburg made it cool compared with many other South African cities.

It was clear the towns that this branch of Joburg's rail network served were connected with gold mining. The great spoil heaps, waste from mining, formed a line of hills only a few hundred yards from the track. This waste had been reworked to recover other valuable elements, in particular uranium. At the time of first mining for gold this element was not on the radar of the prospector and miner

Fred smiled and said to me, "I am impressed with you getting a job with African Explosives."

I surprised and dismayed him by saying, "I am thinking seriously of returning to the UK in the near future."

On that note, after further consultation with Dave about our projected Trans African trek, I finally gave my notice in at the beginning of December. My effective leaving day was on New Year's Eve 1959. I had hoped we would begin our great adventure by the third of January after the hangovers of the New Year had receded.

Treading the boards

Christmas 1959 was not far off. It was a company tradition to put on a theatrical performance using factory staff. *The Pirates of Penzance* was a musical arrangement by Gilbert and Sullivan. They were great Victorian British composers of a series of similar renderings. The *Pirates* was the order of the day that Christmas. I always had an interest in choral music, stemming from my church choir days as a boy in west London. So I decided to volunteer for a part in the *Pirates*. But much to my disappointment it was decided that a policeman would be nearer the mark for me! This involved a number of evenings of rehearsals. The final presentation was scheduled for a few days before Christmas. Naturally this was much on my mind, as I had never partaken in anything quite like it before. It would be performed in the great hall at Modderfontein.

I was nervous about the outcome of this initiative. I would practice my lines, short as they were, in front of the mirror in my room at the Drakensberg Hall. This was done whenever I thought there would be a minimum of inmates resting from their duties.

One young fellow burst into my room and said, "Do you have to keep repeating the same lines? You might not know but some people try to rest in the day time!"

Taken aback I retorted, "I am sorry but I have to get my lines right!"

The country around Penzance, a small town in Cornwall, a county of England, was not only famous for pirates but miners. Many of these migrated to the mines of Johannesburg with the exhaustion of minerals in Cornwall.

Would this tank be used to put down an uprising by Africans?
The author at the top.
Transvaal, South Africa. 1959.

Shortly before Christmas I strutted my stuff in unison with the rest of the company. My truncheon was swung to the beat in my role as a policeman. But this theatre was more than a simple interpretation of Gilbert and Sullivan. It incorporated political innuendoes.

I was never a great theatregoer. However it became clear to me that some playwrights, including the great William Shakespeare, used parody in their plays. They poked fun at the politics of the day, mocked the pompous and drew attention to the injustices of the period.

There were certainly many injustices in South Africa overwhelmingly directed at the blacks. Many of the great confrontations between the Bantu and the South African Police had not taken place during the time I was in the Union. However, there were skirmishes, involving armoured vehicles.

Somehow the producer of the *Pirates* had woven reference to these in our presentation.

It has often been said that the pen is more powerful than the sword. I assumed the musical I took part in was heard loud and clear, well beyond the smoking stacks of Modderfontein. It was well known that the Nationalist government had spies, secret police, in places where talk was not discreet. The English-speaking universities, such as Cape Town, must have been a prime target in this regard.

We got ovations for our efforts and loud laughs at the puns, at the expense of the police and politicians. This must have been reassuring for any aspiring Mandela who might have got a whisper of the dialogue of the *Pirates,* however indirectly. However, there were no blacks in the audience. Mandela and his associates had not been heard of by me at that distant time. Later information revealed the germ of their resistance was already present in South Africa.

The "Good Samaritan"

Christmas was celebrated in the canteen where a buffet and bar had been laid out for the white-collar workers. These included laboratory staff and those from the offices, all white skinned. So Castle Lager and a sausage roll in hand I moved through the milling crowd.

I got buttonholed by a South African industrial chemist who I had not spoken to before.

Hugh said, "I hear you are leaving and that you will be making your way back to London." It was clear he was not interested in my ambitious plans to cross the "Dark Continent," but information about London. He continued, "I want to get a job in London in the next few months."

I said, rather naively, "I will be going back to my home in London." At this his interest took off.

Hugh enquired, "How far is your home from the West End?"

I reflected on this conversation some considerable time afterwards. Young people are not always clear about the machinations of older people at the time. No matter how short an encounter with them might be people would sound you out on the possibility of putting up at your lodgings in London.

The iconic city of London must be near the top of the itinerary of any potential traveller or Dick Whittington. This realisation was reinforced when my Czechoslovak wife and our family paid frequent visits to her country staying with relatives over holiday periods. No matter how distantly related or not even related at all, people would test us out regarding our potential to accommodate them in London!

Some might say I am being very ungrateful when penning these sentiments. After all many people have given me lifts in their vehicles during my treks, even accommodating me at the end of them.

It so happens that my wife and I have accommodated young people we have met on our travels. Invariably having put them up for one week or more we have been phoned by others seeking accommodation and even transport from seaports and airports. These hangers on were not known to us. It is well known that "Good Samaritans" in Britain, be they individuals or governments, have often been taken for a ride in helping others beyond our shores!

Parting dip and sundowner

Christmas Day and a day or so either side was naturally a holiday for the laboratory staff and office workers at my place of work in Johannesburg. But there must have been a limited number of key workers who kept the wheels of industry oiled at Modderfontein's giant industrial plant during public holidays. The dynamite factory involved a host of chemical engineering installations which needed to be kept going 24/7.

During the Christmas holiday I was swimming and lounging around the pool. There was more lounging as I am not a good swimmer. The pool had a backdrop of subtropical vegetation bathed in glorious sunshine and warmth. This encouraged me to sip Castle Lagers until they become "sundowners", to use a South African term for an evening drink. This idyllic spot was on the fringes of Joburg where I spent my last moments with the friends I had made in Drakensberg Hall. One of them had kindly driven us to this memorable location. To spend Christmas in hot sunshine, with not a flake of snow for thousands of miles, seemed unbelievable.

The Boss of bosses

I returned to my laboratory bench after the Christmas break. I happened to be making my occasional walk through the general main lab when I bumped into the Chief Chemist, the bane of one's life. He was accompanied by a shorter, stout, middle aged man, who appeared to be doing a tour of the laboratories. Schwarzkopf greeted me in an unusually affable way. I was not clear whether this was due to the fact that I was about to leave! It could have been related to the season of goodwill, for the New Year was practically upon us.

"Blackcap" introduced me to the stout man as John Brown, the manager of the dynamite factory. I realised in an instance that this was the boss of bosses. My first reaction was to wonder why I, an insignificant laboratory technician, was being introduced to this powerful man. It entered my head it might be an exercise in gloating, almost a joke. Reminding the great overseer of the largest dynamite factory in the world that on my first day in my post my chemical analysis did not hit the target!

But there was no mention of work and the Chief Chemist even deigned to refer to me as Peter.

Schwarzkopf followed up by asking me, "How are you intending to get back to the UK!"

I gave a brief outline of my projected expedition overland across the "Dark Continent."

I said, "I will resort to hitch-hiking whenever possible. I have already several thousand miles of backpacking under my belt. This included over two thousand miles to Cape Town from Rhodesia and my recently completed trek around the Federation of similar length."

Mr Brown's face lighted up into a smile. Whether this was from disbelief or amusement at the seemingly impossible nature of my project, I was not sure.

Schwarzkopf added, "Your performance in *The Pirates of Penzance* revealed another dimension to your character."

I took this as indicating I might have previously come across as a rather retiring person. He probably received reports of me not wanting to join in the card games of my colleagues during the lunch breaks. Instead I buried myself in cowboy and Indian stories of the American Wild West written by Zane Grey. Typical titles were *Riders of the Purple Sage*. A common shrub of this arid area was the sage.

I learnt recently that Zane Grey was a sexual predator taking a host of young women into the purple sage for sexual pleasures. But nowhere in Grey's books that I read did he refer to these erotic adventures. I have heard that such writers are skilled in concealing hidden meanings in their writings. Only those readers practised in such interpretation can decipher such innuendoes. I just treated Grey's yarns as invoking the boundless horizons of the American West before it was tamed by the white man. Cowboys riding into the sunset appealed to me.

Little did I know Red Indian blood would be added to my family from North America five decades later.

So my high ranking colleagues wished me every success in my ambitious project to get back to London the hard way.

Meanwhile my fellow technicians, allegedly busy at their benches, had incredulous smiles on their faces. They cast furtive glances towards my encounter with the bigwigs. No doubt surmising that I had got myself into another fine mess! From that moment I resolved I would send the lab. a postcard from appropriate locations along the route of my trans-African expedition. This would be to prove my latest project turned out to be a success, so I hoped!

African mementoes' magic carpet

Anticipating my final wrench from Johannesburg I gathered together those items that I would need on my impending venture. This seemed more daunting the more I thought about it.

I sewed two miniature flags on the back of my rucksack. One was for the Union of South Africa. This incorporated three even smaller flags. These were the flags of the two old Boer Republics, the Transvaal and Orange Free State, and the other the Union Jack. They deferred to the Afrikaner and British elements in the settling of South Africa. The other flag I sported on my rucksack was the Union Jack.

There were a number of objects that I had accumulated during the time I was in southern Africa. These I could not possibly take on my projected trans-African expedition. Books were among them. They included a set of Churchill's *History of the English-Speaking Peoples*. A volume of this work was sent to me by my eldest sister, Margaret, each Christmas. No doubt this was at the behest of my father.

Unknown to me at the time, Churchill, the aristocratic Second World War leader, was a journalist in South Africa during the Boer War. This was a struggle between the Afrikaners and the British for supremacy in South Africa. He was captured by the Boers but escaped at the end of the nineteenth century.

Even more special than my books was my collection of keepsakes, namely my elephant's tusk and tooth and the leopard carving.

I purchased a large metal box into which this paraphernalia was stacked and secured by a padlock. This box was sent by sea to my family home in West London. There was one item I could not risk by this method of transport! This was my album of diminutive black and whites photos with the occasional one blown up. These were written up in caption form underneath each photo, a record of my escapades in southern Africa.

By a fortuitous coincidence, a miracle in fact, the son of a friend of my uncle, the London Transport underground train driver, contacted me in Johannesburg. Frank was the flight engineer on an airliner of British Overseas Airways Corporation (BOAC), the forerunner with British European Airways (BEA) of British Airways (BA). Frank's plane flew regularly from London Heathrow airport to Jan Smuts' airport, Johannesburg. A growing number of passengers used this mode of travel to and from the Union. They were still a fraction of those that arrived and departed by sea at that time. Flying was an expensive luxury. It was only within the means of a few. No doubt many that travelled in this way were compensated by the fact that they were on business.

So I arranged to meet Frank at a bar in the city centre. Frank was a middle aged affable man of average stature. This meeting was more than just a chat, pleasant as that was, exchanging views of life in South Africa and Britain. It was a chance for me to pass on to BOAC's flight engineer my precious collection of photos of the far reaches of the southern African subcontinent. It was in the hope Frank would transport it, on what seemed to me a magic carpet, to my uncle's residence. Uncle Percy lived on the doorstep of one of the world's greatest airports, Heathrow, London.

Frank flicked through my photo album.

He exclaimed, "What you have packed into your time in southern Africa is amazing!"

"I like to think so. But I did not make my fortune!" I said sadly.

And so it was that my photographic record of life in Southern Africa was eventually restored to the safekeeping of my uncle in Britain. It could be said that my album had an adventure of its own whisked across the sky in a seemingly effortless way. Below the African continent slipped by in less than a day. This route I had ambitions to follow, shortly afterwards, not through the air but overland, a journey likely to last months.

An admirer's anonymous card

I found an envelope addressed to me in my pigeonhole at Drakensberg Hall. Inside was a postcard with the photograph of an assortment of wary wildlife, taking a drink on the edge of a river. This was an iconic, timeless scene, that could, from a cursory glance, have been anywhere in sub Saharan Africa. Judging from the South African species it was somewhere in the Kruger National Park. On the other side was a closely handwritten greeting of remorse that I was quitting South Africa. It wished me a safe and memorable journey across the African continent and back to Britain. It was unsigned! I wanted to believe it was from my fifteen year old Dutch girlfriend, voluptuous Maria, who I had never got close to. This was largely because I never bought a car as she urged me to! However, the handwriting and content seemed too mature to ascribe to Maria.

I doubted the card was from "Sexpot," the plain lady who made sexual verbal advances at me. The origin of this card therefore remained a mystery. There is something appealing about a greeting of this kind. It made me aware that someone would miss me when I departed from a memorable part of the world for one that was thousands of miles distant. This theme would be taken up in the next few days by Dave with whom I hoped to share a great adventure.

ACKNOWLEDGEMENTS

Steven King, PC Kings. Liverpool. IT Support and graphic design.

Nick Lauro, Wirral. IT Support and graphic design.

Dr Peter Farrell, son in law, Wirral. IT Support.

Riverside Writers, West Kirby, Wirral. Constructive criticism.

Charles Cattell, formerly Head of Geography and Geology, Isle of Ely College, Cambridgeshire, England. Constructive criticism.

Dr Colin Gibson, Formerly Lecturer in Sociology, University of London. Constructive criticism.

Mrs Marta Hardy, author's wife, Wirral. Constructive criticism.

Dr Caroline Farrell, author's daughter, Wirral. Constructive criticism.

ILLUSTRATION CREDITS AND ANONYMITY

Photos taken by Peter Hardy, except where otherwise stated. Map designs by Peter Hardy.

Anonymity

The names of persons in my book have been changed.

GLOSSARY

These definitions are as applied to this book. They are not comprehensive.

Acacia.	A tree with umbrella shaped canopy with thorns.
Afrikaans.	Evolution and simplification of an early Dutch language in South Africa.
Afrikaner.	A person of early Dutch settler origin in South Africa.
Apartheid.	Compulsory separation of blacks from whites in South Africa.
A Level	British university entrance qualification.
Assegai.	An African stabbing spear.
Badza.	A substantial African hoe.
Bantu.	Southern Africa black native.
Bantustan.	Region set-aside for self-government of blacks.
Base metals.	Inexpensive metal, such as iron or copper.
Bechuanaland.	A British colony (protectorates) becoming independent Botswana.
Biltong.	Dried meat.

Biogeography.	Study of the distribution of wild plants and animals.
Bioscope.	Southern African term for a cinema.
Blockhouse.	Fort used by British in Boer War.
Boer.	Afrikaner.
Boerwors.	Afrikaner sausages.
Braai.	Barbecue.
Call-up.	Summons for military service (National Service).
Candelabra tree.	A cactus like tree (Euphorbia).
Cape gooseberry.	A person who tags along with an enamoured couple.
Cape colony.	British colony, later Cape Province on creation of Union of South Africa.
Cheer leader.	Person who leads chanting at a rugby match.
Commando.	A group of mounted armed Boers.
Conurbation.	An extensive urban area where a number of towns have merged together.
Corrals.	Circular enclosures for retaining native's cattle, goats and chickens.
Dam.	Southern Africa term for a reservoir. Not the wall.
Demonstrator.	A graduate who assists undergraduates in their university laboratory work.
Dick Whittington's.	Young immigrants with excessive expectations of riches.

Dioramas.	Realistically crafted models of environment in a University rag procession.
Dorp.	Small town in Southern Africa.
Drift.	A ford across a river.
Drum majorettes.	Young ladies in fetching uniforms who enliven a rugby match.
Epiphytes.	Plants not rooted in the ground which grow on trees.
Escarpment.	The steep edge of uplands.
Fallow.	An uncultivated area in a rotation of cultivation.
Fault.	Geological crack in the Earth's crust.
Fetch.	The distance of the open ocean to which a coast is exposed.
Float.	A thematic display carried by a vehicle in procession.
Fool's gold.	Iron sulphide glittering like gold.
Fresher.	New undergraduate student at a university.
Fynbos.	The heathland around Cape Town rich in plant species.
Game.	Wild animals.
Garden Route.	A particularly scenic drive along South Africa's southern coast.
Geomorphology.	The geological explanation of the countryside's scenery.
Great Trek.	The trek (**Groote Trek**) of the Boers from the Cape to the interior of South Africa.
Groote Schuur.	The Prime Minister's residence in Cape Town.

Higher Cambridge.	A qualification for university entrance taken in Southern Rhodesia.
Hottentot.	A non-Bantu tribe encountered by first settlers at the Cape.
Huguenot.	Persecuted Protestant from France who settled in South Africa.
Impi.	A Bantu warrior.
Indaba.	A meeting for debate of Bantu people.
Joburg.	Johannesburg.
Kaapstad.	Cape Town in Afrikaans.
Kaffir.	An early term for blacks, later considered derogatory.
Karoo.	Semi desert occupying much of the north west of South Africa.
Kopje.	A rocky hill.
Kraal.	Bantu village.
Liane.	Tropical plant creeper ascending a tree.
Lichen.	A simple plant resulting from the association of an alga with a fungus.
Lobengula.	Chief of the Matabele.
Location.	A residential area for blacks, often on the outskirts of towns.
Longshore drift.	A current of water moving along a coast resulting in deposition of sediment.
Maquis.	A heathland of Mediterranean climatic areas.
Matabele.	A Bantu tribe in the western half of Southern Rhodesia.

Matric.	Matriculation. Qualification for entry to a South African University.
Mealie.	Southern African term for maize.
Metropolitan country.	The mother country having colonies.
Midlands.	Industrial heartland of Southern Rhodesia.
Monadnock.	An isolated rocky hill.
Mopane.	Tropical tree which casts dense shade and occurs in dense stands.
Mozambique.	Portuguese East Africa.
Nationalist.	The hard-liner Afrikaner political party and government.
Ndebele.	Matabele.
Nyasaland.	Now independent Malawi.
O Level.	English school leaving certificate in 1950s/60s.
Palaeontology.	The study of fossils.
Persona non grata.	An officially unwelcomed person.
Pipe of diamonds.	An underground column of rock containing diamonds.
Poort.	A gap in a range of hills.
Protectorate.	A territory under the protection of Britain.
Rag.	University procession of vehicle borne floats on a topical theme.
Reef.	A gold bearing ridge

Rhodesia.	Shortened version of Southern Rhodesia used in this book.
Roinek.	Afrikaans for an English man.
Rondavel.	A luxurious round, thatched, safari hut.
San.	Bushman.
Savana.	Tropical area of scattered trees, of varying density, in a matrix of grassland.
Serendipity.	Stumbling on fortunate discoveries.
Shebeen.	An illegal establishment were non-whites drink illicitly brewed alcohol.
Southern Rhodesia.	Became Rhodesia at end of Federation and then Zimbabwe.
Soil mechanics.	Soil physics as applied to rocks used in the foundations of roads.
Span.	Harnessed oxen for pulling carts.
Stoep.	Porch
Subcontinent.	That part of Africa south of River Zambezi.
Sjambok.	Rawhide whip.
Slash and burn.	The cutting and burning of bushes and small trees before planting by Bantu.
Tavern of the Seas.	Cape Town.
Tafelberg.	Table Mountain.
Table Cloth.	Cloud which settles around top of Table Mountain.
Tensiometer.	Instrument that measures soil water tension. An aid when to irrigate.

Tissue.	A collection of uniform biological cells for a specific function.
Township.	A native residential area.
Trek.	A long arduous journey.
Tommy.	British soldier.
Transkei.	Area inhabited by Xhosa tribe.
Totsiens.	Goodbye in Afrikaans.
Union.	Union of South Africa.
Union of South Africa.	Union of the British Cape and Natal with the two Boer Republics; Transvaal and Orange Free State.
Veld.	The countryside of southern Africa. Qualified as Highveld etc.
Vesper bike.	Motorised scooter.
Vlei.	Marsh.
Voortrekker.	Early Afrikaner who undertook the Great Trek.
Witwatersrand.	The region and conurbation that includes Johannesburg.
Xhosa.	A native tribe in South Africa.
Zimbabwe.	Ruins of an ancient Shona city in S.Rhodesia, now the Republic of Zimbabwe.
Zuid Afrika.	South Africa in Afrikaans.

About the Author

I was born in central London. Following my eldest sister's birth two years later, I was packed off to my aunty and uncle in Wolverhampton, in England's industrial Midlands. This happened periodically in my early life so that part of my education was in Wolverhampton, over one hundred miles from London. This time overlapped with the 2nd World War. Wolverhampton like London was bombed by the Germans.

My family moved to the greener west London suburb of Ealing in 1938, just before the outbreak of the 2nd World War.

As war dawned we moved to Beaconsfield, a small picturesque town west of London. By this time my dad was away in the Royal Air Force.

After the war we all moved back to our house in Ealing.

I left my small private school aged sixteen with Ordinary Levels in the General Certificate of Education, a school leaving certificate. In spite of no sciences being taught at the school and no sixth form, I got a job as a laboratory technician. I studied Ordinary and Advanced Level sciences in the GCE at the technical college part time, while fully employed for three years.

At nineteen, I obtained a laboratory technician post in Southern Rhodesia, later to become black dominated Zimbabwe. My adventures in Rhodesia are described in Volume 1 of my trilogy. Volume 1 was published in 2020 as *The Gathering Storm, Southern Rhodesia in the 1950s Before Zimbabwe*. ISBN 978-1-78623-672-2 Amazon.

Three years later I hitchhiked from Rhodesia to Cape Town University, South Africa. This enabled me to join the Anglo American Corporation where I tested explosives for the gold mines in Johannesburg. My South African adventures are described in this book, Volume 2.

My work in South Africa was followed by an overland expedition across Africa and Europe. I climbed Kilimanjaro, Africa's highest mountain, and followed the River Nile by hitchhiking and boat.

A Jewish friend accompanied me to Nairobi, East Africa. Then I journeyed alone through the Arab lands and Europe to London. An account of this trek is in Volume 3, published in 2021 as *Riding the Wind of Change, Trans-Africa and Europe Trek, 1960.* ISBN 978-1-83975-534-7.

I gained a London University Bachelor of Science Honours degree, while working as a technician at London University. This enabled me to teach in a College of Further Education, during which I gained two teaching certificates, including one from Leeds University. While teaching in London I obtained a London University Master of Science degree. I finally became an ecologist with a Local Authority, where a council ecological project enabled me to get a Master of Philosophy research degree of London University in my retirement.

I met a Czechoslovak girl in Norway. The following year I married her behind the Iron Curtain, the communist security fence which separated the Russian dominated world from the West. Marta and I have two daughters and six grandchildren. Fifty years later we still enjoy each other's married company in Britain.

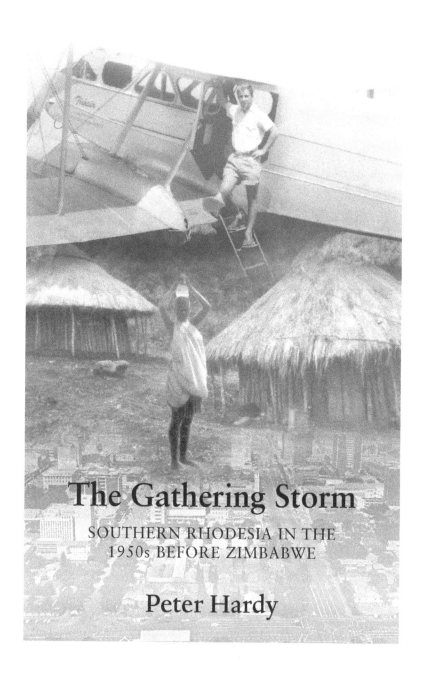

The Gathering Storm

SOUTHERN RHODESIA IN THE
1950s BEFORE ZIMBABWE

Peter Hardy

Riding the
Wind of Change

TRANS-AFRICA AND EUROPE TREK, 1960

Peter Hardy

Lightning Source UK Ltd.
Milton Keynes UK
UKHW010846101121
393713UK00001B/35